The Lady Nurse of Ward E

BY

AMANDA AKIN STEARNS

1909

A nurse's unwavering commitment and dedication illuminate the path to healing. Thank you for being a beacon of hope and strength to those in need.

Col Lana Bernal
2025

COPYRIGHT 2014 BIG BYTE BOOKS

Get more great reading from BIG BYTE BOOKS

Contents

INTRODUCTION 1
PREFACE 2
ARMORY SQUARE HOSPITAL 3
A SCENE IN HOSPITAL WRITTEN 24
AMANDA AKIN STEARNS' DIARY 27

TO

THE VOLUNTEER NURSES

WHO GAVE THEIR SERVICES DURING THE CIVIL WAR TO THE

ARMORY SQUARE HOSPITAL AT WASHINGTON, D. C.

INTRODUCTION

The author of this wonderful and very valuable account of nursing during the American Civil War was born Amanda Akin to Albro Akin and Jemima Thorne Jacacks on Nov. 18, 1827 in Dutchess, New York. She was 34 years old when the war broke out and not quite 36 when she joined the Medical Department of the U.S. Volunteers to work at Armory Square Hospital in Washington, D.C.

The "Sister Gulie" she writes to and refers to is her older sister, Gulielma Maria Akin, one of six siblings.

Throughout her letters and diary, she mentions "Dr. S" or "Dr. Stearns." This is her future husband, Charles Woodward Stearns, born September 24, 1817, and therefore 46 years old when they met. Whether they remained in touch after she left the hospital in 1864 is not clear but on April 23, 1879, they were married in Manhattan, New York City. By this time, Amanda was 49 and Charles was 60. That they had no children is not a surprise.

Amanda filed for an invalid pension on April 8, 1893 as a Civil War volunteer veteran. What her illness or disability was is unknown.

On September 3, 1897, Charles died and was buried in Pawling, New York. Amanda remained in New York and by 1905, was living in a boarding house. In addition to this volume on her war service, she wrote *Ancient Homes and Early Days of Quaker Hill*. Quaker Hill is a hamlet within Pawling. She died on February 2, 1911 in New York City and was buried with her husband in Pawling.

PREFACE

PERHAPS it is not known to many that the Armory Square Hospital was constructed through the desire of President Lincoln to have one as complete and comfortable as could be devised, near the steamboat landing. In 1862 he called D. Willard Bliss, Surgeon, United States Volunteers, from a Michigan regiment, to organize a system of general hospitals in and about Washington. One result of his coming was the speedy erection of this one, on Government land, about the Armory, opposite the Smithsonian grounds. All of Dr. Bliss's far-seeing suggestions and ingenious, though simple, arrangements to aid in caring for the sick and wounded were discussed weekly with the President. So later the hospital came to be considered the most complete and best conducted institution of its kind during the Civil War. By the spring of 1863 Dr. Bliss had gladly accepted the offered services of a sufficient number of ladies to serve as nurses, one for each of the ten wards, when gradually the professional or paid ones had left. A special diet kitchen was built with funds contributed by their Boston friends, and early in 1864, at President Lincoln's suggestion and with his practical assistance, flower beds were arranged between each of the long barracks, which proved indeed grateful to tired eyes and weary hearts. He came often to visit the hospital and shake hands with the soldiers, always with a kind word, when his eyes had a sad, far-away look, and he often paused before those suffering most intensely to utter a warm "God bless you."

A. A. S.

AKINSIDE, QUAKER HILL, N.Y

September, 1909.

ARMORY SQUARE HOSPITAL

WASHINGTON, D. C., April 28, 1863.

MY DEAR SISTERS: You are no doubt anxiously looking for a "sign of life" from me, but I can tell you initiation into hospital life of such a novice is not lightly to be spoken of, and until my ideas ceased floundering and I could recognize my old self again, I could not trust myself with a pen. The feeling of a "cat in a strange garret" has now quite left me. With the first effort the work took hold of me so firmly that my own identity seemed for a time lost. It is inexplicable why I should have come here, and how easily I have fitted in the place.

Arriving at Washington 6 P.M with my uncle, who could not persuade me to wait until morning, we entered the hospital at the general office (the only opening from the street). I boldly asked the surgeon in charge at the desk for Dr. Bliss. "He has gone home," was the curt reply. After telling him who I was, as if some one ought to be expecting me, I asked for Miss Platt, the only one I knew. He gave me a quizzical look through his spectacles, and for reply said to an orderly nodding in a corner, "go and find Miss Platt." Saying to my disgusted relative, "It is all right; I understand. Good night," I followed my guide, with a courage born of necessity, through loosely boarded passageways, coming out at the back of the long whitewashed wards, where the convalescents were sitting outside (to me then a grim-looking lot), until we came to Ward C, at the entrance of which we met Miss P—, with hands full of some patient's supper, which on seeing me she gracefully handed to an attendant, and welcomed me to her room, an enclosure boarded off from the convalescents' " grub " room, when I was thankful to feel that I had arrived.

As the supper hour had passed I seemed to be an "elephant" on everyone's hands, until a young woman nurse, who shared the room—Miss Hill, of Belmont, Mass.—came in, and taking in the situation began "mothering" me, and never ceased until, in spite of "red-tape" regulations, she brought me some supper, and had another iron bedstead, etc., put in that room. I shall never cease to call her "Mother" Hill. Being slightly refreshed I assented to Miss P—'s invitation to go in her ward, when she went to make her last rounds and give out the night medicines. I meekly followed through the long ward, unable to return the gaze of the occupants of twenty-six beds, to the table in the center, and with a sinking heart watched her raise the head of a poor fellow in the last stages of typhoid, to give him a soothing draught. Could I ever do that? For once my courage failed. On returning, my friend informed me the man could live only a few hours, and as they were carried out soon after death I must not be disturbed if I heard them, and saw the lights the other side of our partition. That was sufficient to keep my already overstrained nerves tense until they passed, and I saw the lights winding to the House of Death. After that, exhausted, I slept through my first night in a hospital.

With the morning came new life. Surgeon-General Bliss was early in his office. I reported to him, and was soon installed as nurse in Ward E. Our ward master, "Jobes," a Pennsylvania boatman, with wife and children at home, beamed a welcome at me on every occasion, and when the surgeon in charge of the ward (my quizzical friend of the evening previous) came to visit his patients and did not notice the newcomer, Jobes took the first opportunity to say, "This is the lady who is to have charge of the ward," the only reply we received, accompanied with a little nod, was "Humph!" evidently not approving of a lady's presence in a hospital. As you can imagine, that touched my mettle, and was a good tonic, so I went to work. Having ascertained that he was from "way-off " Erie, Pa., I said to myself, " He will find out what a determined young woman from New York can do." As there had been no woman in the ward for a week the big-hearted "Jobes's" unsystematic ways were evident on all sides. For the first two days it rained incessantly, and I looked at Miss Platt passing to and fro from Ward C with a smiling face, humming to herself, in astonishment unable to see aught but satisfaction in trying to relieve the suffering and discharge my duties properly; but since I have become a part of the system, it is another thing.

It is like the solar system: every ward revolves on its own axis, with its own surgeon, nurse (feminine), No. 6, or orderly for both, ward master, cadet surgeon to dress wounds, three attendants and two night watchers—all together revolving around Dr. Bliss, the surgeon in charge. The "reveille" sounds at 6 A.M., and we have just time to dress and arrange our rooms before we go to our wards to dispense the medicines, which is a responsible part of our duties. Then come the breakfast for the men, to the dining room attached to each ward, and the *special diet* for those who cannot leave their beds, which the nurse, with the assistance of her orderly, gives out according to the doctor's prescription. Every bed is numbered, and the men are so designated. After our own breakfast, we meet the surgeon in our ward, who makes his prescription on a card hanging by each man's bed. His orderly brings the cards to our table for us to make the orders for medicine and send to the dispensary, or if for *special diet* to send them to that kitchen. The medicine chest is placed upon a table in the center of the ward, which also contains the stimulants, our especial charge, of which we keep the key; alongside it are our own table and chair, that being our special post.

Besides our regular morning duties there is the constant supervision and care of so many worn and suffering, and yet so grateful patients; letters to be written, etc. One poor boy in our ward, without a relative in the world, has made many friends here. He has daily visitors and presents from outside, and no one thinks he has too much. He has been confined to his bed for eight months with a wound from which at times he suffers intensely, with very little hope of any improvement. He never complains, but is ready with a merry laugh at the doctor's jokes.

We again dispense the medicines, etc., before 12 au., the hour for the men's dinner. As the hospital now is not crowded, the engagements of late having been in the South, we get a few hours for rest or a walk before 5 P.M., when we resume our duties at the medicine chest, etc. We spend the evenings trying to entertain our men (Mother Hill calls them boys).

At a quarter to nine, when the night watchers come, we give our last directions and retire. "Jobes" says, "The men have got quite a liking for me already," which may sound strange to you, and would be better understood if you saw the respect so universally paid to us. We pass up and down among these rough men without fear of the slightest word of disrespect. They feel their dependence upon us for comfort and entertainment, and the difference in the wards where there is no "lady" shows how much can be done for them. In one ward (C) there is a melodeon a kind friend sent to Miss Platt, and the convalescents are very happy to have the ladies come and sing with them.

Our cadet surgeon told me to-day that he was musical and could play on three instruments by ear, and we have one "stuttering" man who, sitting up in bed, his wounded limb having kept him there two months, sings by the hour and makes jokes for all about him. I do not write of the sad things which occur daily and hourly before me, and to which it seemed at first I should never get professionally accustomed. Although there are so few in the hospital, there are deaths every day. A strong, able-bodied man who accidentally shot himself is in our ward, life and death struggling with him for the mastery. He is a German, and as he is a stranger to all, he scarcely speaks. I wrote a letter for him to his wife, for which he was very grateful.

The hospital is pleasantly located opposite the Smithsonian Institution grounds, now beautifully green; with the Capitol on the other side, though at a little distance, its elevation brings the fine building in full view. You will understand we are in barracks, the walls of rough boards, papered inside, but still comfortable. There are men to sweep, to attend to the fires, etc. We have other volunteer nurses, among them may be mentioned Miss Lowell, of Boston; Miss Low, niece of Senator Hale, of New Hampshire; Professor Felton's daughter, of Cambridge, and Miss Griggs and Miss Marsh from Massachusetts. We meet at table in the rough room Dr. Bliss has had arranged so that we could be apart from the general dining room; but we have not the leisure to be very sociable. There has been a little "earthquake" here since my arrival, which revealed to the volunteer nurses that we were under army regulations. Dr. Bliss was suddenly arrested and taken to the Capitol jail, and an army surgeon put in charge of the hospital *pro temps*. It so happened that the next day was pay day for all the soldiers and employees of the hospital. Imagine our virtuous disgust and indignation on being called to the general office to receive a month's pay for our service! We had to take it, being a small elephant on the officer's hands, to which later we became for the day reconciled, and went to market to select some treat for our boys. The upheaval was brought about by a dishonest steward, who had been discharged by Dr. Bliss, and who reported some pecuniary embarrassments of which he had knowledge, etc., to Secretary Stanton, and got an order for Dr. Bliss's arrest. You may imagine the consternation, a *silent uproar*, though outwardly all was calm. Senators Hale and Chandler were telegraphed for. Miss Platt and Mrs. Ingersoll (widow of the Attorney General of Maine) went to Surgeon General Hammond, to the provost marshal, and lastly to Charles Sumner, and to Secretary Stanton himself. So Dr. Bliss is liberated on parole, and demands an investigation. Of course, there was great rejoicing when he returned to the hospital, and probably there will never be a time to call it up again.

Though writing hurriedly, I hope I have given you a clear impression of the life to which I have devoted myself for the present, as I could not remain at home inactive when there was so much need of service.

Always assured of your affectionate interest and sympathy, I am,

Lovingly,

YOUR SISTER.

ARMORY SQUARE HOSPITAL, WASHINGTON, D. C.,

May 14, 1863. MY DEAR SISTER GULIE: I must first tell you that my trunk arrived safely yesterday, and you may believe the pleasure it gave me was not alone from its contents, but the sisterly interest and care shown in everything. Tell Annie the hat is a beauty, but a little too fine to go through the general office. However, it is needed for church, and other times, and the old one will serve when we go out in haste after supper for a little walk. We can go to church only on Sunday evenings as the mornings are occupied by the weekly tour of " inspection," when Dr. Bliss with his staff of ward surgeons, head clerks, etc., pass in procession through the wards, every man by his bed, and we at our posts. You will find this letter to be a hurried and disconnected one.

Since the wounded from the battle of Chancellorsville have arrived, our life has become very exciting and absorbing. I write anywheres, in ward or room, for the moment, with mind on many other things. If I had written last Saturday or Sunday I would scarcely have been able to speak of anything but our poor wounded soldiers. We looked for them the first of the week, and when the heavy ambulances went past in procession, taking those least wounded to more remote hospitals, I, at least, became possessed of an undefined dread. On Thursday morning at daybreak *they arrived,* about one hundred and fifty, and on Friday one hundred more. The sound of the general ward master's bugle took us out of our beds. I shall never forget the scene as we looked from the window into the darkness, only relieved by the lanterns in the hands of those waiting to receive them, as the ambulances were driven slowly up one by one, and their burden carried in either on a stretcher or between two men, if only the lower limbs were injured. My friend had already "wrestled" herself into her clothes, and I did not tarry. The wounded had been put in haste on the floor, on chairs, anywhere, but all nervousness was gone when I saw their brave hearts reflected in the faces of those able to sit up. One man at once arrested my attention; he was sitting by the stove, with one foot covered with bloody cloths, drawn over his knee, his clothes torn and soiled, telling some listeners about the battle in exciting terms, with his bright black eyes glistening, and forgetting the loss of two or three toes! Even the severely wounded men who could speak were cheerfully waiting their turn to be bathed and put in bed, thankful to get to such a comfortable place. Poor fellows! many of them had been shelled *out of three* hospitals after they were wounded, and as one said to me, "were obliged to 'skedaddle,' even if they had but one leg." One poor fellow brought in our ward was so blackened and burned by a powder explosion that some one remarked, "There is not much use bringing him in," but on dressing his burned face we found his eyes had been protected (probably by his hands, which were fearfully burned), and that he was determined to live. When we consulted as to whether he could take food, he very quickly answered beneath the plasters which covered his face, that he could eat if we would put something in his mouth; his jaws were stiff because he had had nothing to use them on, since he was wounded on Sunday. You may believe not many minutes passed before I had a cup of hot coffee and toast, pushing it into his mouth in the best way possible. His feeding was my special care for some days; he always knew my voice, and when I did not come he would tell the attendant "he wanted his mother to feed him." Since the bandage has been occasionally lifted from his eyes, I think he feels disappointed in not finding me as motherly looking as he expected.

Time will not permit to tell you more. Suffice it to say, they are a brave, noble set of fellows, and with scarcely an exception bear their great sufferings without a murmur. There has been but one death in our ward; there was no hope for him when he came. The ball had passed through the spine and paralyzed his lower limbs, so we could not regret when he was relieved from suffering.

Perhaps I ought not to write you these sad details, but they have absorbed my mind completely, and I know your thoughts and hearts are equally and deeply interested in this fearful war. It is most interesting to hear the men conversing and comparing notes about the battle. One Zouave boy, about eighteen, says to a friend, who had hobbled in from another ward, "Why, I thought you were dead. They said your head was blown off," and then both fell to talking about it in an amazing manner. Their wounds had been dressed as well as could be expected, hurriedly in a field hospital, not neglected as the New York *Herald* reports. They say "Joe," as they call General Hooker, "is *the* man, and that he is a brave and good general." You probably receive the war news nearly as soon as we do, and probably with more details. "Stonewall" Jackson is dead. Hooker has been reinforced, and has recrossed the river. Our hospital is thronged with visitors after 1 P.M. Secretaries of relief societies are looking up the men belonging to their States. Mothers are looking for their sons; sisters for their brothers, etc., etc. It is a little world by itself, but the same God rules over all, and we are thankful. A gallant old gentleman in Congress (brother of Owen Lovejoy, the noted Abolitionist) was introduced to us by Mrs. Ingersoll.

He says, "We can take care of the soldiers, and he will take care of us," so he comes quite often to accompany us in a walk after supper through the Capitol grounds. He writes verses, and is a friend of Mrs. Sen. Lane. Tomorrow evening, for diversion, he is to take a party of us to another hospital, where they have theatrical entertainments. Miss Platt's married sister is in town and will go with us. Dr. Jenkins, of Yonkers, came in to see me before leaving. You know he has been actively connected with the Sanitary Commission, and his wife was with you in those successful charades Mrs. Livermore arranged for the benefit of the soldiers. One day I was glad to meet the Rev. F. W. Ware, of Boston, whom I failed to see when I was invited to his house near the city by his wife's sister, Miss Rice. I like Miss Felton very much. She sent to my ward yesterday a half dozen games and puzzles for my men. Mr. John Ware had sent her a quantity, and she was glad to share them.

The New England ladies here are constantly receiving valuable boxes of good and useful things, which are dispensed liberally. Miss Hill has furnished Miss P—and me with all the condensed milk, wine, etc., we need at present. Please tell Annie to send half worn shirts, neckties, etc., to put in my box. Our attendants think it a great thing to get a white shirt for Sunday, and you know, poor fellows, they soon leave them behind when transferred. Through Jobes, I received a compliment from our old surgeon this morning. "He was glad they had changed matrons. I was worth a dozen of the one who preceded me." It has made me feel quite proud as you may remember he received me with a nod and a "Humph." Please tell Mrs. Hamilton that the men in my ward favorably received me because I was thought to be a *McClellan* woman, and yesterday I was called to the ward master's room and presented with a plaster figure of the general, which I have had placed on a bracket (made by one of the men), over the door, which called forth an expression of disapproval from my radical Boston friend, Sister Griggs, who said " McClellan is doing nothing but organizing an army." Precious little I know what he is doing, but I told her if my sick or maimed soldier boys had been under his command, and wanted it there, it would remain. No politics in the army!

Many kind letters come for me often, which are very comforting. Mrs. Secretary Wells and a friend come often to our ward, and assist me in writing letters for the men; there is so much to be done after a battle. Many come offering to assist, but their lack of sense or officiousness, and sometimes their mischief-making, oblige us to be very circumspect.

The Smithsonian grounds opposite are such a treat to us. We can run there for a few moments, and the complete change renovates mind and body.

The weather now is fine; a few days are very warm, so that the men lying in bed suffer much.

With much love to all,

Affectionately,

YOUR SISTER.

ARMORY SQUARE HOSPITAL, WASHINGTON, D. C.,

June 13, 1863.

MY DEAR SISTER: It seems to me, as day after day passes with its unceasing round of duties, that the time for writing home will never come. If the hour or so of leisure on which we count in the afternoon is taken up by something unexpected, either of pleasure or care, whatever we have appointed for it must be deferred. When we come to our rooms unusually weary, Sister Hill or I make a cup of tea (Sister Platt makes the coffee), and we discuss hospital affairs over it, which for the last fortnight have been exceedingly interesting since our Dr. Bliss has been reinstated. This life is one of constant interest and excitement, like a journey through foreign lands. The scene constantly changes, the principal actors and conveyance alone remaining the same, and the important feature of one day is obliterated by the one equally so of the next. I should regret very much that I was not keeping a journal if I did not know it would rob me of necessary rest. It is late now; there goes the "night watch," and officer of the day making their rounds, and old Mason says, "There's a light in there," but it is my surgeon, Dr. Stuart; so there is no danger of my being reported. I was determined to make a commencement to-night on this sheet, which has been waiting for me a fortnight. I feel the want of time for letter writing or scribbling in my journal as much as any sacrifice I am making, and should dearly love to write hospital sketches. To-day being Saturday, I had my medicine chest to arrange for Sunday's inspection, which detained me in my ward after dinner; then a letter to write for a poor wounded soldier (who will probably not live) to his mother. He was wounded in a cavalry skirmish and brought here from Culpepper night before last. Then followed a short but interesting conversation with him about his past and rather reckless life, and his hope for the next; then a cooling drink for Jobes and some of the attendants, who had been scrubbing and scouring for Sunday; a little conversation with stuttering "Joe," who has been suffering from a swollen throat, having taken cold since he has laid away his crutches and gone out on a pass; then a slight rebuke to Tommy, an old man attendant, who is a capital nurse, only he insists, occasionally, on giving medicines which the doctor has not prescribed. Now and then strays in "Scott," the former bugler, now in the dispensary, a right pleasant fellow, who wishes to borrow a piece of music to practice on the bugle, and I must needs go and try it on the piano, which now occupies a conspicuous place in the center of our ward, the only one in the hospital. Scott is very fond of music, so I have made his acquaintance since the piano came. Then the time arrived to give out medicine, and the afternoon was spent, leaving me only a few moments to change my dress for supper. On leaving my room the general ward master's call sounded, which announced that more wounded had arrived, and everyone was on the alert in a moment. One hundred wounded came; they were the most severely wounded from the battle of Chancellorsville, and they have been lying six weeks at Potomac Creek and have now been sent here through fear of the rebels reaching there.

[The battle of Chancellorsville, fought from April 30 to May 6, 1863, in Spotsylvania County, Virginia, near the village of Chancellorsville, was a Confederate victory, often attributed to the loss of never of Joe Hooker. Stonewall Jackson was shot by his own pickets by mistake and died a few days later.]

The same routine must be followed before the poor man is put to bed: his card made out and hung at the head of his bed; his clothes, which are taken off, made into a parcel, labeled for the knapsack room; and an account entered in the ward master's book, which in Ward E is kept by the "lady nurse"—an agreement between Jobes and myself, he being not much of a bookkeeper; as he has always insisted upon taking charge of the night medicines (mostly pills and castor oil), I readily assented to have him continue in charge. It is not every nurse here that has a Jobes, who when Father Wilson at the cookhouse protests that "there are too many special diets on Ward E's list, and he will have to report the nurse there," tells him "to go to the d—l," and makes out the diet list himself, and "he can report *him*"; Jobes must swear a little, though he has the kindest heart imaginable.

Good night, I must go to rest.

SUNDAY, JUNE 14TH, 2 P.M.—Hooker and his army are "skedaddling" as fast as possible—at least the sick and wounded are. One hundred more wounded arrived here this morning, about 4 A.M. Everyone had to fly, surgeons and all. For a time all was confusion—reports, with the new ones included, to be made out. Everything paused with surprise until finally one wheel set the rest in motion. As there was no diet requisition made out for the new arrivals, there was a "skirmish" in getting something for them to eat. My head is filled with prescriptions and diet lists. These last arrivals were mostly from Aquia Creek, which has been deserted. It is sad indeed to see so much suffering and sacrifice of all that makes life dear, and nothing accomplished toward putting an end to the rebellion.

It is a great advantage to have a room at the end of one's ward, and when Dr. Bliss returned I applied for it, as we were still three in one room. He consented, but a girl from the linen room had taken possession of it, and it required an order from Dr. Bliss, through the general ward master, to get her out again. Fearing I would get the "blues" from the lead-colored army blankets tacked on the floor, I walked out and bought some matting. Jobes assisted me in getting some furniture here and there from the Quartermaster's stores, etc. (I have been in the army long *enough not to question)*, and now feel that I have a *home* here. As every door must be opened Sunday morning for inspection, my self-respect rose, when Dr. Bliss, at the head of his train, paused a moment at my table, on his return through our ward, to say approvingly, "You have made a great improvement there."

Some friends of Miss Lowell in Boston have given three hundred dollars toward building a separate house on the grounds for the "lady nurses" (as we are called), and Dr. Bliss says it shall be done at once, trusting for more donations if necessary.

Some friends came in, one evening, accompanied by a man with a fine tenor voice, to sing for us. I wish you could have seen how the soldiers enjoyed his medley songs.

SUNDAY, 4 P.M.-I cannot write long without interruptions. We have short religious services in the wards on Sunday afternoons. The chaplain, with others from outside who wish to speak to the soldiers, pass from ward to ward; the melodeon goes with them, and Sister Platt plays the hymns when there is no one to relieve her. I always expect to be in Ward E when they come, both for my own comfort and the example to others. The soldiers join in the singing, and the most careless are glad to hear a prayer for their wives and children. I have been to church only twice, but comfort myself in thinking if I do not hear much preaching, I am trying to practice what they preach.

SUNDAY, 9 P.M.-Oh dear me, the cry is "Still they come!" and we are overflowing; they come now without order, and are received with but little ceremony. Our forces are obliged to retreat and have already made bonfires at Falmouth, and as soon as all the wounded can be removed will probably do the same at Aquia Creek. Those who have arrived say it was distressing to see the confusion and the efforts of the wounded, to get to some means of transportation. It seemed to me this evening, as I sat at my table adding to the list of medicines—writing down, name, regiment, list of clothing, etc., of the new arrivals, calmly looking at the poor maimed sufferers carried by, some without limbs, on a "stretcher"—that I had forgotten how to feel, and when I went to the open door and glanced upward to Night's glittering mantle, it seemed as if I were entirely separated from the world I had left behind. Certainly, "I am not myself at all."

While I write, and it is very late, there is a constant rumbling of ambulances, or loaded wagons passing, cars are whistling, bells ringing, trains coming and *going*. I suppose you will hear about the possibility of the rebels reaching Washington; they were fearful of a raid at Alexandria last week, only six miles below us, and set up defenses. But I must not write longer. Good night.

MONDAY EVENING.—It is surprising how soon the new arrivals become accustomed to our order of things, and soldier-like, while suffering, are on the lookout for something to "drive dull care" and sharp pain away. Since I have rented a piano which stands in the center of the ward, you would be amused to see your sister at the piano, and our Dr. Stuart with his violin (we are now on the best of terms), a respectable crowd of soldier boys behind us, playing all kinds of jolly melodies, and later the plaintive ones, which we tell our wondering neighbors, prepares our patients for sleep better than their soothing medicines. Of course, when receiving newly wounded, or the suffering is too acute, and all are too occupied and weary, or a soul is trembling on the verge of eternity, it is forgotten and out of place.

But I must go to rest; with one loving thought of home which embraces you all.

Affectionately, YOUR SISTER.

ARMORY SQUARE HOSPITAL, WASHINGTON, D.C., June 28, 1863.

DEAR SISTER: Fearing you may get anxious when you read to-morrow's papers I write a few words this morning. We have been much amused with some of the headlines of the New York papers, but for the last few days it has looked gloomy here, and to-night we have some palpable proofs that the rebel heads are turning this way. Two men were brought into Ward E this afternoon, wounded this morning in a cavalry skirmish only six miles from "Chain Bridge." They say the "Rebs" shouted "they intended to take breakfast in Washington to-morrow." The soldiers say "they wish the Rebs *would* throw some shells into Washington to wake up the Cabinet, and make them show more activity and earnestness, or give it up entirely." It seems to me either Jeff Davis himself or the other "ould boy" has taken the reins of government in his hands.

As you can imagine there is much excitement here, not that they expect Washington to be taken, but the necessity of doing *something*. There is constant signaling from the Capitol, and we hear bugle calls and wagons leaving town, but this is only what is expected when our troops are moving. Our little hospital world goes on as usual. I have not yet told you of President Lincoln's visit to our ward a fortnight or more since. It was pathetic to see him pass from bed to bed and give each occupant the warm, honest grasp for which he is noted. I hear that he is especially interested in this hospital, and has suggested having flower beds made between the wards with plants from the Government gardens, which Dr. Bliss is having done. His homely face with such sad eyes and ungainly figure did not fill my youthful idea of a "President of the United States"; but it was a grand thing for him to come and cheer our soldier boys with his presence. No doubt the fearful responsibility of his office weighs heavily upon him.

Two more volunteer nurses have arrived, so the last paid ones will be relieved to-morrow. One is to be my roommate, Miss Southwick from Boston, daughter of P. R. Southwick, a leather merchant. She has been in a hospital at Alexandria for a year, so is quite an old soldier in the service. She has added a small cheap bureau to our room, and given me two drawers of it, so we fraternize nicely. One day last week I was favored by a visit from Lieutenant W. G.

Dickson, Headquarters, north of the Potomac, a friend of Miss Sherman, who had written him an introductory letter, and he had come to see if he could be of service to me. Yesterday one of his orderlies brought me an exquisite bouquet of rare flowers with his card.

Yesterday we received a patient formerly from New York City, now one of General Heintzelman's clerks. He left a position in the American Exchange Bank to join the army (George Shephard). He is not very ill, and he has not put on hospital clothes; his bed is near my desk, so he often comes and helps himself to special diet, and we talk about New York because we can.

Our good old Dr. Stuart was very ill last evening. He has most severe attacks of rush of blood to the head and almost loses his senses. He depends on Jobes to care for him. I ventured in to see him last evening as he called' for some tea, and he was glad to have me assist in holding his head, while Jobes "cupped" the back of his neck.

I received Mrs. Brewer's (wife of Rev. D. R. Brewer of Yonkers) parcel of flannel shirts, etc., remaining on hand when the society disbanded, and our attendants in Ward E are delighted with the scarlet shirts. They wear them under blue flannel blouses, and are proud of them. Please send all that I requested, as we do not expect to be upset here by the rebels—our hospital is too important an institution. Don't forget the cake as my appetite wavers, and many days I take my tea and a piece of cake for dessert.

MONDAY, 11 A.M.—The "Rebs" did not come to take breakfast with us, and we did not wait for them. I have made out the morning report for Jobes, also the medical officer's report, and "Ramsdell," the head clerk (since he has found out who has arranged Jobes's book), says he thinks of having me transferred to the General Office. Each wardmaster's report was called for, so the surgeons could make their reports. Jobes's book, which I found *incoherent,* to say the least, I rearranged, and have continued to keep it, so it is one among the very few which is satisfactory, and *Jobes is very proud of it.*

How do you like my long rambling journal letters? They tell me that no mail leaves Washington to-day. I hoped to have sent this before any obstruction came. Perhaps you had better defer sending me anything until you are sure the mails and express can go through. As there is no more fighting at present, our ward is comparatively quiet. Last week it was whitewashed and some improvements made in the rear. This week we are to have new mosquito nets. Sister Platt has a very interesting patient, a young lieutenant, wounded in the head, whose life, or at least his reason, she saved by sending post-haste for the leeches, which the doctor prescribed, and which could not be furnished in the hospital. He is now convalescent, or sufficiently so to be moved. His sister, Mrs. McKinley of Philadelphia, has come to take him home. Being somewhat at leisure I joined her and Sister Platt in a morning visit to the White House and Capitol. We saw the fine statue which is to be placed on the dome of the Capitol, the new Senate chamber, etc., etc. The grounds are beautiful, but so far we cannot get to them often. Now comes the old man to tune the piano and renew the rent, and Jobes follows in a few moments, handing me five dollars, contributed by Dr. Stuart and the men; they are so anxious to keep it. Please thank Will Ogden for the papers received this morning. The men are looking at them now, and often buy papers brought in the ward. I was much interested in a letter written by Mrs. Swissholm from "Campbell Hospital" in the New York *Tribune* Uncle J sent, as I received the lemons in our ward from her hand, and was glad to know her impressions.

MONDAY EVENING.—This is a perfectly splendid evening, and, with Sisters Hill, Platt, and Marsh I have been enjoying it from the window of Miss Platt's room while our bugler gave us some sweet music. Forgetting the red tape around us we applauded, and at the same time watched the signal lights from the dome of the Capitol, causing a strange ebb and flow of feeling, alternate joy and sadness, a strange mixture of thoughts of peace and warfare.

Lieutenant Dickson came to see me again this evening—is he not kind? He is so dignified, yet always agreeable. It is a great pleasure to see and talk with him. He assured me that Washington was not in any danger of being disturbed, though the rebels passed within four or five miles of these fortifications last night on their way to Harrisburg. The report to-night is that McClellan is called to take Halleck's place; that Stanton is superseded by Butler and Hooker by Meade. Once more let us have *faith!* I believe Father Abraham and his advisers have been pretty well frightened, and will now put aside personal ambitions and politics, or is it simply inexperience?

My journal letter goes on as could not mail it to-day. When Will O— thinks it is safe to send it, I would like some money in Government bills. New York money is refused by some people here.

I am writing partly because I do not wish to retire yet. Dr. Stuart is out, in town. Jobes wished to go out—something unusual—and there is a man in the ward who has been deranged all day, and this evening is quite wild, so I have taken the responsibility of giving him some medicine without a prescription, and wait for their return.

Let me hear from you immediately. Affectionately,

YOUR SISTER.

ARMORY SQUARE HOSPITAL; WASHINGTON, D. C.;

August 7, 1863. DEAR SISTERS: I was delighted to get your letters, but you must not expect me home quite so soon. I do not think I can leave before September, although our duties are light and the hospital goes on in a quiet, methodical manner. Dr. Bliss goes to Boston next Monday, and Miss Lowell accompanies him. He wishes the rest of the ladies to remain until he returns—then *our house* is to be finished about that time, when I could choose a room and attend to the moving of our few belongings, leaving Sister Southwick to keep house. I should prefer not to return until there was need— about the last of October —and must not ask for too long a furlough, if I wish to retain a right to my own ward.

AUGUST 10TH.—The weather is exceedingly hot, as you can easily imagine, even with a breeze. Fortunately, we have very little to do in our wards. The attendants are faithful, yet the patients still in bed look wistfully at us when we leave. They want something to keep them cheerful. A few days since, the beds not needed during the day were all put out of doors for an airing, and we had only seven who could not be moved. The poor boy with typhus fever died a few days after the fever turned, when we thought his life was to be spared. His father arrived only in time to take his lifeless body home, which was embalmed, as all the soldiers are who die here. He blessed No. 6 and myself over and over for our care of his dying boy, and gave us the wine, etc., he brought for him. All the other fever patients are convalescent. In fact the whole hospital is so comfortable, *comparatively,* that I tell them we are becoming *gay* and dissipated.

We have had a number of pleasant things to enjoy during the past fortnight. The anniversary of the hospital was celebrated last Saturday, and we had a very pleasant evening. Ward F was decorated with flags, evergreens, and hanging baskets of flowers; the beds were taken out, seats brought in, and a platform arranged at each end—one for a band of music, the other for Dr. Bliss, the distinguished guests, and the chaplain, who presided. Representative [Francis William] Kellogg from Michigan made a fine, humorous speech, informing Dr. Bliss that he was the recipient of seven cases of elegant and rare surgical instruments, valued at $480, which his friends in the hospital wished to present to him as an expression, etc., etc., and Dr. Bliss made a charming little speech in reply, in which, as a matter of course, he alluded so beautifully to the ladies here that afterwards one old gentleman said to him, "he did not know of which he was most proud, his new instruments or his lady nurses." There was music by the band; then J. M. Edmunds of the Land Office made a short speech. Mrs. Fowl, an accomplished singer, gave us "Red, White and Blue," all joining in the chorus. After the crowd dispersed, Dr. Bliss, who has a fine tenor voice and belongs to a musical family, with his brother and niece sang for us. We have little extempore concerts in the ward now quite often, as we have found among our patients two good violinists, a pianist, and one to play bass viol. You will wonder how there can be any gayety or amusement among so much suffering. That is all borne and seen, as unavoidable, and anything that will keep them from despondency, and will not add to anyone's sufferings is welcomed with pleasure.

I send you a letter written by Walt Whitman for a Washington paper descriptive of one of these little concerts the soldiers enjoyed so much.

A soldier's life is one of strange contrasts, to which it was difficult at first for us to become accustomed. One afternoon we had a "reading" in the ward by the Hon. Mr. Lyon, "The Prisoner of Chillon," and poems by Thomas Hood, which I at least enjoyed.

Among other interesting events, one night a *baby* arrived. A wife of one of the soldiers, who came to see her husband, gave birth to a fine boy at the chaplain's house on the night of her arrival. Our surgeon, Dr. Stuart, was called, and the child is soon to be christened "Stuart Jackson" for him and the chaplain. The mother had no clothing for herself or child, but soon received enough to last a year. We all prophesy he is horn to be a soldier.

We have enjoyed two long drives in Dr. Bliss's Michigan wagon; an account of which I send you in rhyme, as Sister Southwick insisted on my writing it out, promising " to do something for me while I was writing "—your old offer repeated.

The other drive was still more interesting. We, Sisters Platt, Hill, Southwick, and I, had a nice ambulance and driver, according to an order from Dr. Bliss. Being obliged to go to the Provost Marshal's Office for a pass, we sent in our driver with Dr. Bliss's written request to get one, but word was returned that we were all to go in, for which our surgeons try to tease us, saying it was not at all necessary. The office was filled with clerks and dignitaries, and you may believe we had some jokes among ourselves. I whispered to Miss Platt, rather louder than was necessary, that they ought to tie a *piece of red tape* around each of our necks, and if they did not describe us as pretty good-looking we would not sign the paper. We drove over the "Long Bridge" into Virginia, "ole Virginny," and many miles to Fort Corcoran and Fort de Kalb, where Sister S— has a friend (Mrs. Colonel Tannat), her husband having command of the fortifications. He gave us a pass to go inside, and we were obliged to show it to three before we were allowed to enter. Then an orderly showed and explained everything to us, which was of great interest. On our return at sunset we had a most beautiful view of Washington and Georgetown. We crossed the bridge to the latter, and returned that way. The roads in Virginia were worse even than "corduroy," and on our return from the fort we were obliged to hold on to one another.

I must also tell you of a new acquaintance, George Wood, Esq., author of "Peter Schlemyl," etc.

We often now spend an evening at Mrs. Irving's. On one occasion, a fine-looking, middle-aged gentleman with gold-rimmed spectacles came to me, and commenced an interesting conversation (rather sentimental I thought at the time) about our hospital, etc., at the close of which he said he should do himself the pleasure of coming to see us. I did not know who he was, and thought no more of it, until later he came to my ward with Sister Griggs, who had met him before, and introduced himself as an author, etc. He expressed much interest in our anticipated anniversary, and accepted our invitation to attend with pleasure. Another noted author, Walt Whitman, visits our hospital almost daily. He took a fancy to my fever boy, and would watch with him sometimes half the night. He is a poet, and I believe has written some very queer books about "Free Love," etc. He is an odd-looking genius, with a heavy frame, tall, with a turned-down Byronic collar, high head with straggling hair, and very *pink* rims to his eyes. When he stalks down the ward I feel the "prickings of my thumbs," and never speak to him, if not obliged to do so, though I hear some of the other ladies offer him a cup of tea, which he enjoys with the relish of a little talk with them. With all his peculiar interest in our soldier boys he does not appeal to me.

Sister S— and I have just now a pleasant companion—a sweet, pretty girl, just from boarding school—Miss Fox, sister to a major who was brought into Sister Southwick's ward a fortnight since in a critical condition, but is now doing well. They belong to a clergyman's family living near Rochester. She is the only daughter and has four brothers in the army—one a chaplain, one a major, another a captain, and the last a lieutenant. The major is very pleasant. He sent me an "enigma," having arranged it to pass away the time, which I solved and took to him in Ward H last evening, and enjoyed a very pleasant talk with him.

The weather is so exceedingly *hot* and our wards are in such a comfortable condition I regret that I cannot be at home now, and we nurses are tempted to go to Point Lookout on the seashore, or to Gettysburg, where nurses are needed, and we would have good mountain air, but fear Dr. Bliss would never forgive us. However, the few weeks will soon pass. I shall be so happy to be at home and see you all again, and perhaps remain into October.

With love,

Affectionately yours.

A SCENE IN HOSPITAL WRITTEN

BY WALT WHITMAN, 1863.

I MUST give you a scene from one of the great Government hospitals here. I go to them every day to inspirit the drooping cases, and give the men little gifts, sometimes of articles, sometimes of money. Two or three nights ago, as I was trying to keep cool, sitting by a wounded soldier in the Armory Square Hospital, I was attracted by some pleasant singing in an adjoining ward. As my soldier was asleep I left him, and entering the ward where the music was, I walked halfway down and took a seat by the cot of a young Brooklyn friend, S. R—, badly wounded in the hand at Chancellorsville, and who has suffered much, but who at that moment in the evening was wide awake and comparatively easy. He had turned over on his left side to get a better view of the singers, but the plentiful drapery of the mosquito curtains of the adjoining cots obstructed the sight. I stepped round and looped them all up so that he had a clear show, and then sat down again by him and looked and listened. The principal singer was a young lady nurse of one of the wards, accompanying on a melodeon and joined by the lady nurses of other wards. They sat there making a charming group with their handsome, healthy faces, and standing up a little behind them were some ten or fifteen of the convalescent soldiers, young men, nurses, etc., with books in their hands, taking part in the singing. Of course, it was not such a performance as *Medori or Brignoli* and the choruses at your New York Fourteenth Street Academy of Music take a hand in; but I am not sure but I received as much pleasure under the circumstances sitting there as I have had from the best Italian compositions, expressed by world-famous performers.

The scene was indeed an impressive one. The men lying up and down the hospital in their cots (some badly wounded—and, perhaps, never to rise thence), the cots themselves with their drapery of white curtains, and the shadows down the upper and lower parts of the ward; then the silence of the men and the attitudes they took — nothing to interrupt the singing—and the whole combination was a sight to look around upon again and again. And there sweetly rose those fresh female voices up to the high, whitewashed wooden roof, and pleasantly the roof sent it all back again. They sang very well; mostly quaint old songs and declamatory hymns to fitting tunes. Here, for instance, is one of the songs they sang:

HOMEWARD BOUND

Out on an ocean all boundless we ride;
   We're homeward bound—homeward bound;
Toss'd on the waves of a rough, restless tide,
   Yet homeward bound, homeward bound.
Far from the safe, quiet harbor we've rode,
   Seeking our Father's celestial abode,
Promise of which on us each He bestowed,
   So we're homeward bound.
Wildly the storm sweeps on us where it roars,
   Yet we're homeward bound;
Look! yonder lie the bright heavenly shores,
   Where we're homeward bound.
Steady, o pilot, stand firm at the wheel;
Steady! we soon shall outweather the gale;
Oh, how we fly 'neath the loud-creaking sail,
   As we're homeward bound.

As the strains reverberated through the great edifice of boards, it was plain to see how it all soothed and was grateful to the men.

The singers went on; they sang "Home, Sweet Home," and a beautiful hymn called "Shining Shores." I saw one of the soldiers near me turn over and bury his face partially in his pillow; he was probably ashamed to be seen with wet eyes. Since I have mentioned it, let me give a verse or two:

SHINING SHORES

My days are gliding swiftly by, and I, a Pilgrim stranger,
Would not detain them as I fly, those hours of toil and danger;
For oh, we stand on Jordan's strand, our friends are passing over,
And just before, the shining shores we may almost discover.
We'll gird our loins, my brethren dear, our distant homes discerning,
Our absent Lord has left us word, let every lamp be burning;
For oh, we stand on Jordan s strand, our friends are passing over,
And just before, the shining shores we may almost discover.

Such were the fine and vivifying songs these girls sang there for all our sakes, until quite late in the night. The sounds and scene altogether have made an indelible impression on my memory.

SOLDIERS, TALKS, ETC.

Soldiers you meet everywhere about the city, often superb-looking young men, though invalids, dressed in worn uniforms, and carrying canes, or, perhaps, crutches. I often have talks with them, occasionally quite long and interesting. One, for instance, will have been all through the Peninsula campaign under McClellan, narrates to me the fights, the marches, the strange, quick changes of that eventful campaign, and gives glimpses of many things untold in any official reports or books or journals. These, indeed, are the things that are genuine and most precious. The man was there, has been out two years, has been through a dozen fights, the superfluous flesh of talking is long worked off him, and now he gives me little but the hard meat and sinew.

I find it so refreshing to talk with these hardy, bright, intuitive American young men (experienced soldiers with all their youth). The vital play and significance of their talk moves one more than books. Then there hangs something majestic about a man who has borne his part in battles, especially if he is very quiet regarding it when you desire him to unbosom. I am continually lost at the absence of blowing and blowers among these old-young American milltaires.

But in the hospitals I have talked most with the men for months past. I have found some man or another who has been in every battle since the war began, and have talked with them about each one, in every part of the United States, and many of the engagements on the rivers and harbors, too. I find men here from every State in the Union, without exception. (There are more Southerners, especially Border State men, in the Union army than is generally supposed). I now doubt whether one can get a fair idea of what this war practically is, or what genuine America is, and her character, without some such experience as this I have had for the past seven or eight months in the hospitals.

AMANDA AKIN STEARNS' DIARY

November 4, 1863. LEFT home for Washington, returning to my hospital duties—a fatiguing day's ride on the railway, though from Philadelphia I was enlivened by the interesting conversation of a gentleman who asked the privilege of occupying the half of my seat. After finishing our papers and taking a slight nap I concluded a little conversation would relieve the embarrassment of such a close proximity, and saw that he was very politely waiting for me; so I ventured a remark, and when the ice was once broken, conversation did not cease until we reached W—, when he escorted me to the car, and left it at Seventh Street to put me on the one which passed Armory Square Hospital, where he bade "Adieu," with a "God bless you," and "Happy to have met you." I wonder *who* he is! Received a pleasant welcome from friends at the hospital and from my *soldiers* in Ward E. My bright-eyed Johnny—the "Pet," so young and winning, when the spasms of suffering were over—was not there to greet me, but I pray God is awaiting me in heaven. My hospital sisters took me to our "chateau," and Sister Southwick found some supper for me at the chaplain's, after which we went to Ward B, where Sister Platt was presiding at one of her little evening concerts to amuse the patients.

November 5, 1863.

Miss Low retained my ward until evening, giving me an opportunity to unpack. After dinner I rode in ambulance to the "Dismounted Camp" with Sisters Southwick, Griggs, and Hill, and Drs. Draper and Banister, which gave us a very good idea of the front. "Dahle," former Orderly, who had been at the hospital only two days before I returned, and reported himself at the camp, recognized the establishment and came to meet us. We inspected their hospital cooking apparatus, tents, officers' quarters, which were very nicely arranged, and last but not least, tasted their coffee which "Dahle " offered us after cleaning a cup. On my return reported to Dr. Bliss, who gave me Ward E, and sent word to Miss Low to report to him. Mr. Ramsdell came in with a pleasant welcome in the evening.

November 6, 1863.

Spent most of the day in my ward; I find my Philadelphia student (who is acting "No. 6" while Patterson is at home on a short furlough to vote) very companionable and agreeable. Sister Hill came in for a little talk in the evening. Mr. Ramsdell also called (I don't know what for), though he said "to see if my hair was arranged differently," as he protests against the change—the new "Waterfall."

November 7, 1863.

Endeavored to get my ward in order for to-morrow's inspection. Mrs. Secretary Welles and her sweet niece came in the afternoon; they welcomed me so cordially with a kiss I was much pleased and shall avail myself of their kind invitation to visit them. Played over some of my music on Miss Felton's piano. Wrote until very late—commenced a journal letter for my sisters at home.

November 8, 1863.

Not one hour for quiet meditation. Miss Platt was absent spending a week with Mrs. Colonel Whistler at Fort Corcoran. "No. 6" and I were invited to join our choir and follow the melodeon through all of the services in the different wards, which lasted until five o'clock. In the evening I attended the Episcopal church on Seventh Street with Sisters Southwick and Griggs, and Dr. Banister.

November 9, 1863. I was aroused about three in the morning by our "orderlies" coming for the keys to our medicine chests, and giving information of the arrival of the wounded from the late engagement at Rappahannock Station, where they say our troops have gained a victory, but oh! at what a fearful price. I never witnessed such suffering be-fore—such frightful wounds. Nine died on the way here, one also very suddenly in our ward. I made him some toast water which he took from my hands and drank, thanking me for it, then went to my supper; when I returned in about twenty minutes his bed was empty. Although suffering severely he showed such a meek and quiet spirit, I feel confident that he inherits one of God's gracious promises—"Blessed are the meek." I was completely occupied all day, using my leisure moments to write letters for the men, conversing with visitors, who throng the hospital—retired weary with the sight and sound of suffering and saddened with the thought of finding another empty bed in the morning. May God have mercy on the poor sufferers!

November 10, 1863.

Another empty bed as we feared, and one of our lieutenants, wounded near the lungs, breathes as if his hours were numbered—Lieutenant Waite of the Sixth Maine; the other one, Lieutenant Potter, wounded in the arm, is very comfortable. Mailed a letter for home to-day.

November 11, 1863.

I was excited and delighted this morning to find Lieutenant Waite much more comfortable, conscious, and able to take nourishment; his cousin, who is in the Quartermaster General's office, is staying with him. He showed me this evening the *carte de visite* of the Lieutenant's sister and the lady to whom he is engaged, both beautiful and very interesting in appearance. What agony they must suffer! Am happy to record my "etagere" has been painted and varnished, so I can commence to put my ward in order. I was delighted to see Dahle, who called at "The Chateau" this afternoon, and related to me his experiences since he left W, which were very interesting as he has been in active service. I hurried to the ward to attend to "Special Diet." Spent the rest of the morning in Ward F, where we had the melodeon, some singing, and the violinist.

November 12, 1863.

Beautiful day. "One of summer's jewels which she let fall when gathering up her treasures to depart." Had lunch en *tamale,* at the "Chateau"; I was surprised to hear from Miss Felton that James Gibbons, a brother of my old teacher, Professor Gibbons, was the author of the "New Gospel of Peace." Read a very ludicrous and characteristic letter from Walt Whitman to his "fellow comrades," as he called the soldiers. As they failed to understand the jumbled sentences written on foolscap, they brought it to me. He was spending a vacation with his mother in Brooklyn, and his love for them was repeated in many incoherent sentences. I could only imagine it was written very late at night and he had taken "a drop too much." Had a long and satisfactory conversation with Dr. Bliss about the "Special Diet." Lieutenant Waite's brother arrived.

I mended my bags in the evening. They are so serviceable. They were a happy thought of our friend, Mrs. Livermore, through whom I offered my services to Dr. Bliss. They were made at her suggestion by our church sewing society at Yonkers, N. Y., to button over the top of the iron bedstead, in which the occupant could keep his toilet articles, home pictures, etc. I was surprised by a call from Dr. Robbins, who has left Pittsburg and who is again waiting for an opening at Armory Square.

November 13, 1863.

Lieutenant Waite died at six o'clock this morning; what grief for those two young hearts I Enjoyed some fine music in Mrs. Wilson's room, by the Captain of the "Invalid Corps," doing guard duty.

November 14, 1863.

Being Saturday I have been more than occupied. Had my canary brought from Ward H. Arranged my *etagere*, the shelves and table on which rests my medicine chest, and the ward generally, until nearly five o'clock. Found Miss Platt at the "Chateau" and chatted awhile with her. After tea proposed having music in our ward, as we have so many patients in bed, but Miss Marsh insisted upon having it in hers. Mr. Ramsdell came in and spent an hour with me, then we went to find Sister Hill, who was in G, with the music. It is raining furiously, and "No. 6" borrowed an umbrella and came home with me.

November 15, 1863.

Inspection as usual, our ward pronounced "perfect." Funeral services for the Maine men (nine in number) were held in the open air; the Flag which they had so nobly defended was draped over their coffins and wreaths of white flowers laid on their breasts (which are to be sent home to their relatives). The chaplain and others made a few remarks, and all the Maine people and agents in town followed, with many from the hospital, in carriages, to the soldiers' cemetery. Attended the Wesleyan Chapel with Dr. Baxter in the evening, whom I found conversable, and enjoyed my walk very much.

November 16, 1863.

Found my Philadelphia student acting orderly ill in bed, with an abscess forming in his throat, which would have been quite serious for me, as well as himself, if my old "No. 6" (Patterson) had not returned. I made and applied poultices all day to his throat, without losing my presence of mind, like the heroine of Fannie's story, who could not remember where it was to be put. He amused and entertained me very much, and we could not resist joking even when he could hardly speak. Mr. Ramsdell passed the most of the evening in my ward, which made an otherwise dull one very pleasant.

November 17, 1863.

Found my especial patient somewhat better, the swelling having broken. Received a call from Surgeon Smith, who had in his charge all the officers outside of the hospital and visits those at the chaplain's daily. He had also in his care Clara Okell's father, who is dangerously injured, and came to tell me that she was with him and would come to see me perhaps to-morrow. I went in to see Colonel Millett, as Mrs. Jackson, the chaplain's wife, insisted; found him very cheerful and agreeable. Dr. Baxter came in also, and it is unnecessary to repeat my favorable impression of him. Found a wee little *mouse* inside of my packing trunk and invited "No. 6" down to punish him for his presumption; he also took a large picture which I brought from home to the ward and hung it very nicely. After dinner I invited my Philadelphia friend to accompany me to the "Chateau," or "Shamoh" as he calls it, as he was still feeling miserably, and thought perhaps the sight of a comfortable room and chair would do him good. Gave him some cherry brandy and cake, taught him to play backgammon, so he returned quite refreshed. Lovely Indian summer weather; but could not make the exertion to take a walk; played backgammon in the evening.

November 18, 1863.

An anniversary which made me quite thoughtful, and perhaps a little sad. Miss Okell came to see me with Surgeon Smith. It was delightful to see a face from Yonkers. I went into the chaplain's to wait for her escort, who was still busy with his distinguished patients, who afterwards came in and chatted awhile. The chaplain as usual offered a few jokes. Attended Miss O— to the ambulance, while Dr. S— paused to have a conversation with Dr. Bliss, whom we met. Waited a few moments after giving out "Special Diet" to see the men paid. Friend Conyers came to the "Chateau" and tacked up my curtain. I found his note of thanks with his now useless bandage on my table. It grieves me to see my noble-hearted "49" suffer such intense agony, and makes me restless and determined to have something done to alleviate it, though I fear amputation will alone suffice. Went with Friend C— to Miss P—'s ward to hear the music, but she had decided not to have it there this evening, so called on Miss Griggs and Dr. Banister and arranged an impromptu concert in Ward A, which the patients seemed to enjoy very much.

November 19, 1863.

Feeling quite indisposed I yielded to Miss Griggs's persuasions to consult Dr. Alcan. Requested a special pass of Dr. Bliss for Conyers, to accompany the ward master and assist him in selecting clock, etc., for our ward, as he had collected over thirteen dollars, with which to make improvements. Received the riding skirt from Miss Okell by Dr. Smith. Mrs. and Miss Irving called. I intended to go out and select a piano, but felt weak and nervous (something unusual for me), and after the ladies returned to their wards I enjoyed the delicious quiet of the twilight and the fading sunset behind the varied and fanciful architecture of the Smithsonian. There was not an interruption but one —the boy who brought my tea—until a short time before "taps" Miss G— and Dr. Banister came in; but I had no spirit for conversation and retired behind "the scenes," or screen.

November 20, 1863.

I passed a miserable night and did not leave my bed until my breakfast was brought, of which I could eat very little—the toast being tough and sour. Although feeling very weak I have spent an unusually interesting day—in fact, our little reception room was not without visitors from 9 A.M. until 4 P.M., though I retired to my room at three. In the morning my friends here called—Conyers, Miss Irwin, Mrs. Wilson, Dr. Stuart (who came professionally), and Johnny Hegeman, who returned last night, and Mrs. Jackson, by whom I sent some pickled plums to her two interesting patients, and Dr. Dexter. At dinner time Mrs. J— brought me some very nice pudding, though Mrs. Wilson had sent me an abundance, for which I had a very good appetite, not having had any breakfast. At I P.M. the escort and band of music came to take Major Wheeler's body (of the Fifth Wisconsin, though late of Boston, and which has been lying in state in a tent put up for it yesterday soon after he died) to the train. His sweet young wife sustains herself beautifully under her great grief, but was quite overcome when the lieutenant of his regiment came to the door of our little room to find her, as we had invited her and her friends to sit here while waiting the arrangement of the ceremonies. Sister S— opened the door of our bedroom, that she might rest a moment in seclusion and weep unrestrainedly. When the body was placed in the hearse, the low, solemn music of the band was very impressive. The bodyguard stood on either side, with their bayonets reversed; the large escort were outside the gate, and when the hearse and carriages had passed out, it moved on in sad procession to the dirge-like music. Colonel Millett, to whom I sent an invitation to share our window, as he is too much of an invalid to stand, was as agreeable as usual. Immediately after the procession left Dr. Draper came in, soon followed by a lady (Miss Smith), who belongs to an old family here and is quite a character, I should imagine. Her conversation was most fluent and cultivated, which I enjoyed exceedingly, although I could not coincide with some of her opinions. In expressing her bitter sentiments against Secessionists, she included her own sister, and forgot the Christian charity which we are taught by our blessed Saviour's example and precept to cultivate above all things. Our French surgeon, Dr. Alcan, made us the last call before tea. Fortunately I had retired. Mrs. Jackson brought me my tea, which was so good and homelike that it turned my thoughts thitherward. Mrs. Wilson sent me some supper, too, which I gave to the guard, who was then pacing up and down before the window, and the poor fellow's gratitude gave me double pleasure. The ladies returned home early, and a Mr. Pond, from the Treasury Department, accompanied Miss Griggs and spent a half hour. I retired early.

November 21, 1863.

This was one of Beecher's rainy days, "pouring with a good will," so there was no going to my ward, and to tell the truth I did not feel much like it. Dr. Stuart, Conyers, and my ward master each paid me a formal visit this morning. After dinner the ladies assembled in our little reception room, according to "Special Order" from Dr. Bliss to meet him, but the hour passed and he did not keep his engagement. I have since heard he was ill and that he went home.

We read Edward Everett's splendid oration at the consecration of the National Cemetery at Gettysburg. The prayer by the chaplain of the Senate (Rev. Mr. Stockton) was sublime, and our President's brief remarks were more than eloquent and worthy of the occasion; so we all sewed and read and had quite a social meeting, else I would have been very lonely this dismal day. Augustus brought me my tea and a bowl of nice oyster soup, which I divided with the guard pacing up and down in the rain, and I enjoyed his part as much as my own, when he returned the bowl by the open window looking so well pleased. Miss Platt came in early, and I was delighted to see her, having played "solitaire" quite long enough; it was very fortunate that she did, for the stupid guard (not the one to whom I gave the oysters) let a drunken man pass belonging to one of the wards, and seeing our light, concluded to call; but Miss Platt sprang to the doors and locked them, so he went on and I gave the guard a short lecture (professionally).

November 22, 1863.

I dressed at my leisure, not wishing to go to my ward until after inspection, and called on Mrs. Jackson and stayed until I saw the train of medical officers pass out. I enjoyed a chat with the two patients, who were agreeable as usual. Spent the day in my ward, as I could not expose myself to the damp earth, and was unwilling to remain a prisoner in the "Chateau." I found one of my soldiers very weak from hemorrhages and Dr. Stuart vainly endeavoring to keep off one of his violent attacks of headache, so kept moving about, determined that another surgeon should come to attend our patient. I increased his stimulants and succeeded at last in getting Dr. Keenan here. Had a very pleasant conversation with No. 49. After reading to him a chapter from the New Testament, I attended services in Ward F, where we had quite an interesting speaker; the Baptist choir was also present, but our chaplain was absent. I was too much fatigued to go farther after reporting to Mr. Green, who conducted the services, that we could not have him in "E" to-day. I returned to the ward and read a sweet little poem, "Charlie, the Drummer Boy," aloud to some of my soldiers gathered about the stove, who seemed very much interested. I went with Conyers to Ward C, to assist in singing and then home thoroughly fatigued.

November 23, 1863.

Miss Griggs accompanied me to select a piano. I was so fortunate as to find one, but she will be obliged to wait a week as pianos are in such demand at this season. I bought a pretty lamp, also, for our ward. I was obliged to rest a while, before going there, on my return—I am so weak since my three days' indisposition. I arranged to send ambulance and men after the piano, and sent Dr. Stuart after the pass for them. Conyers is so full of spirits, keeps us all lively, and amuses me greatly. I spent the afternoon with Sisters Platt and Griggs sewing and chatting, more of the latter. This was a musical evening; two officers (captains), formerly in Ward F, came from Georgetown, where they were transferred to officers' quarters which they do not like at all, after their comforts here under Sister Hill's supervision, and being musical they sang and played on the melodeon. We went to hear them and invited them to come to Ward "E," and the audience followed. Miss Platt, Conyers and others sang.

Cross, a patient in Ward C, and some one else played violins, with Curtiss accompanying them on the piano. Mrs. Wilson's eldest daughter (who, by the way, is very pretty) also joined us, so we had quite a concert and inaugurated our piano in "E."

November 24, 1863. This was a rainy morning, and feeling miserable, sent for my breakfast. I had just reached the ward and was making out "Special Diet" fortunately, when Dr. Bliss came in prepared to find fault with our special order for milk; but being at my post, I was able to explain satisfactorily. I practised my music after dinner, which I enjoyed much; wrote in my journal, played backgammon with patients, and had music in the evening. No. 39 quite comfortable—in fact, we had given him so much punch and it was so strong that he was inclined to be talkative. There was melodeon music and singing in "C," but I declined the invitation to join. Received a letter from home this morning, which raised my drooping spirits, but was disappointed because they fail to order my *carte de visites*. I was amused, however, by the news generally, particularly that of the three engagements, and of the purchase of a town house: What next?

November 25, 1863.

I was in my ward all day, and was very busy. I cut the paper for ward master and Conyers to put over the windows where the old fringe was torn, which annoyed me so much all summer. New stoves were put in the ward. Two of our worst cases were removed to "I," which is also in Dr. Stuart's charge at present, and two others to "K," as Dr. Bliss is at last sensible of the fact that we had more wounded than any other ward, and too many for the good of the patients, so feel quite relieved of care. After dinner I found Sister S— suffering from severe headache; gave her an emetic, etc. I made arrangements with "N. York Relief man," who is to furnish Miss P— and myself with oysters and cranberries for our soldiers on Thanksgiving Day (tomorrow). When I returned to my ward I found Conyers finishing the paper, and as No. 6 went out I took Johnny H— for orderly, who assisted me in framing some pictures, gave out the medicines, etc. There was music for an hour.

THANKSGIVING DAY, November 26, 1863.

The unclouded sky and exhilarating atmosphere were types of the sunshine and joy in hearts made glad by a holiday. Our soldiers seemed to enjoy their freedom and the good things prepared for them, and as that is the one especial object to which we are devoting ourselves at this time, we were happy too. We also had a fine dinner for which we were thankful, not having fared very sumptuously of late; Dr. Alcan having kindly remembered us by sending some of his nice French cordial with his compliments, we made ourselves quite merry with toasts, the first being to Dr. Alcan's health, "Long may he wave," offered by Miss Platt, to which Miss A added, "Before the grass grows over his grave"; the second to "Our Surgeon in charge"; the third, "The Laziest Surgeon in the Hospital"; the fourth, "Mrs. Gray, who sends us such palatable 'Special Diet' for our soldiers"; the fifth and last, to "Mr. Wilson: may he live to provide us with another Thanksgiving dinner, and as much longer as his wife desires."

The band of music I enjoyed exceedingly—it was just the sunset hour. Mr. George Wood, the author of "Gates Wide Open," otherwise styled, "Peter Schlemyl," called for the first time since my return, and accompanied Miss Griggs and myself to the "Reading in H" by Miss Harriet Fanning Read, in whom we were disappointed, though I enjoyed as I should anyone who read comprehensively one of Shakespeare's plays. Sister Southwick presented me with "Hospital Sketches," by Louisa M. Alcott; Miss Marsh treated us with Boston mince pie at the "Chateau" in the evening, over which we gossiped a while before retiring.

November 27, 1863.

With regret we said "Good-by" and parting good wishes to Dr. Baxter, who goes to the front. Dr. Stuart did not make his morning rounds, so we took our duties quite leisurely. After dinner I supplemented our scanty meal with coffee and mince pie at the "Chateau," having with me Sisters Platt, Southwick, Hill, and Marsh. This was a pleasant day in my ward, as no one was suffering severely, and everything glided along smoothly. Miss Thomas came and sang for the patients while I was at the house; in the evening I played backgammon with No. 6, wrote in Miss Platt's letter to Dr. Bowen after perusing his to her. Conyers escorted me home, where we found quite a party, Drs. Stearns and Robbins taking coffee with the ladies. [Dr. Charles W. Stearns was Amanda's future husband.]

November 28, 1863.

This was another dark, rainy day. Retired to the "Chateau" with a sick headache. Mrs. Jackson, hearing I was ill again, came in, prescribed for me and brought in some homelike toast and tea. Miss Griggs being confined to the house also with a sore throat, we could converse over the partition which separates our rooms, and I was entertained by the conversation between her and Dr. Banister, her surgeon, who is really the most sociable, agreeable, and conversable surgeon I have met here. The ladies reported a very fine concert in my ward. Miss Thomas sang to quite a crowd, and as she is young and pretty, the soldiers enjoyed it very much.

November 29, 1863.

I took breakfast with Sister Griggs at the "Chateau," went to my ward just before "inspection," and did not return until evening. It gave me pleasure to be able to obtain a special pass for Conyers, who wished to dine with his cousins; talked with No. 48 for an hour to make him forget that he was suffering (and believe he did) listening to him while he was describing their part in the storming of Mary's Height, and keeping the enemy in check at the battle of Chancellorsville, and crossing the Rappahannock in small boats, etc. The Honorable Mr. Lovejoy came in with the wife and daughter of a senator (I believe from Illinois), with whom I had a pleasant conversation, and who offered her services if they could assist me during the winter. I met Mrs. Irving and Mr. Ashton White in Sister Platt's ward.

November 30, 1863.

I went with Sister S— to hospital nursery to select plants for our window shelves, then to ask Mrs. Sampson of the Sanitary Commission to intercede with the surgeon general, and ask that our "dresser" might be retained as all the Ohio soldiers are to leave tomorrow. I was pleased to hear that Colonel Wysworth from Yonkers has charge of the Invalid Corps and is in town. The mother and brother of No. 48 arrived unexpectedly and his delight gave me much pleasure to witness. As they were strangers and knew not where to find a lodging place, the old lady proposed remaining by his bedside all night, which being against the rules I took Conyers home with me to ask Sister S— to take a spare bed in Mrs. Ripley's room, so I could occupy hers and give mine to the old lady, for which she was very thankful.

I found the ladies somewhat excited and in consultation with the General Ward Master, as "Uncle Ben" had exerted himself so tremendously to get our house warm, the furnace pipe was red hot and we were fearful it would ignite the floor; a little management soon subdued it, and we passed a quiet night, with the exception of Sister Hill, who required some mustard paste, which lulled her again to forgetfulness.

December 1, 1863.

Dr. Bliss appointed another meeting of the lady nurses at the "Chateau," and again disappointed us. I found a note from Henry (our dresser), who was obliged to leave, and did so without saying " Good-by " to anyone, he feeling so moved that he was obliged to write it. I regret exceedingly that I did not go to Colonel Wysworth *en personne*. Miss P— spent part of the evening in Ward E, there being music and chatting generally.

December 2, 1863.

Dr. Smith called and insisted upon my going to see Miss Okell. I concluded to ignore my headache and go, and as his ambulance was at the door, I called for her to accompany us to see the head of the bronze statue of the "Goddess of Liberty," which crowns the dome of the Capitol, placed on her shoulders, which event took place at twelve o'clock. Mrs. President Lincoln was there in an open carriage, with nothing particular to mark her from the occupants of the other carriages, but a pug nose and a rather severe expression. The crowd cheered immensely as the head of the statue reached its place. Cannon announced the fact to the fortifications about Washington, which saluted her each in turn. I went in the Capitol to see the new bronze doors, which of course are fine, the cost being thirty thousand dollars. Our dinner hour being passed when I reached home, I took my little teapot to "Special Diet Kitchen" to make some tea; I found Mrs. Gray there, who very kindly gave me some toast, and I enjoyed it ever so much in her little back room. Dr. Stuart introduced a Mr. Perley, who wished some music, thus opening a conversation about the present to be given to Dr. S—, proposing that I should receive the money, both from our ward and his company, the President's bodyguard, which he represents.

December 3, 1863.

Finished letter for home. Clara O— came for me to go to the Smithsonian, which I enjoyed, though I returned chilled and tired. I talked with her about our hospital life, etc., in which she seems much interested and promises me something for Christmas for my soldiers from Yonkers. Unfavorable news from our unfortunate Army of the Potomac. There was a hospital concert in Ward C.

December 4, 1863. One month since I came here, and it seems more like three. I framed pictures to decorate our plain brown paper walls and remained in my ward after dinner until three o'clock as No. 6 was out and many of our convalescents feel the effect of the mild weather, or the change, and have taken to their beds with fever and severe headache. Conyers came in with such a headache that he could scarcely see. He came to our "Home," as I promised him some homeopathy and cologne to bathe his head. I arranged my dress and hurried to the ward, found that Johnny Hegeman, in whose care I had left the keys, had given out the medicine. He is really quite bright and useful. He enlisted under age, and was brought here very ill with fever before the regiment reached the front. Arranged my ward for the concert, which passed off splendidly. Borrowed Sister Hill's lamp and bouquet for the piano and was quite proud of its appearance. We had a feast of music, which I enjoyed with the soldiers to the utmost. Mr. Martini, who played very sweet and spirited accompaniments on the piano; Mr. Parsons, whose voice is superb, so musical, and natural; Mr. White and two others, whose names I forget, and Miss Kitty Irving, so *petite* and pretty, played two pieces, altogether the most successful concert we have had yet. Mrs. Irving, Mrs. Dean, and White accompanied and the ward was crowded. There were no bad effects visible to-night.

December 5, 1863.

Fine weather! Went to the House after dining, made my toilet for Saturday afternoon. Dr. Banister vaccinated me when he came for Miss Griggs, as I was informed at breakfast that I had a case of "varioloid" [a mild form of smallpox affecting people who have already had the disease or have been vaccinated against it; Abraham Lincoln had it in the White House] in my ward; gave Dr. S— my opinion on the subject of his not telling me when he suspected it. Conyers came to the House, as I promised to read to him, he was feeling so miserably, and did so until five o'clock. Mr. R— came in a moment to show me an amusing little contraband image some lady had made for him. After tea Johnny H— insisted upon taking up the glass basket, Sister Gulie's offering, made of beads, and No. 6 suspended it, which proves quite ornamental. Miss Thomas came and sang in the evening, bringing a crowd again to the ward, attracted as much by her pretty face as the music. I omitted to mention Major General Hancock visited our hospital—a noble-looking man.

December 6, 1863.

Found my worst predictions verified in poor "Denser," whose head I had bathed, etc., and he with the other case, whom the surgeon had suspected from the first, were sent to the "Kalorama Hospital." A sad day altogether. My suffering patient, 48, asked Dr. Bliss to examine his foot, which he consented to, after dinner, and finding the bone materially injured, amputated it. Conyers suffering all day with such a neuralgic pain in his right temple and eye, was obliged to keep chloroform and opium on it and when evening came and I was sitting by him to keep him from feeling lonely and dispirited, thoughts of home came very sweet and its comforts seemed very far off; read aloud a chapter from Miss Alcott's "Hospital Sketches," which seemed to entertain a number very much, particularly my sensible John, lying in the next bed to Conyers, who said he did not see where such an interesting book came from; he had not been able to get such and would like to buy it. Retired quite early for me.

December 7, 1863.

In the morning the visit of the Russian Medical Staff was the all-important topic, except that Miss Griggs and I agitated ourselves about being present at the opening of Congress, which I would have preferred, but knowing it would be doubtful about our getting through the crowd, and finding Conyers had passed a miserable night without sleep, saying he thought I would never come in, put everything but ward duties out of my mind, until I had things in order for inspection, special orders written and signed, No. 48 attended to, and C— somewhat comforted, though I tremble to write, we all feared for him, the dreaded visitor, which has taken two of our number to the "Kalorama." At this moment Dr. Smith came in, saying Miss Okell and others were waiting at the door for me to accompany them to Alexandria. I knew the sail and fresh air was just what I needed, and having arranged things to my satisfaction, I said yes, glad to run away from inspection, even though it brought the Russians, and get the fresh breeze and relief for my anxiety. We took the boat at the wharf and a half hour's sail brought us to A. Walked to the "Wolfe E. W. Hospital," where were two friends of Dr. Smith, wounded and brought there last week—Colonel Higgins of the Eighty-sixth New York and the "fighting chaplain," as he is called, Mr. Barbour, from Troy, with a severe wound in his leg. He was so handsome and agreeable we were quite charmed; asked us for our autographs. From there to St. Paul's Church Hospital to see young Dr. Allen, formerly of Ward E, whom I promised to visit. Unfortunately he had just left, and we were obliged to hurry to the boat, which left at I P m. Said "good-bye" and home messages to Miss O, found Sisters Southwick and Griggs just returned from the Capitol, but were unable to get in for the crowd, so went to dinner together, but as usual did not find much. Hurried to my ward with my little teapot of tea; wrote letter for No. 4S, informing his mother of the loss of his foot. Spent a sad, anxious afternoon by C's bed, who was burning with fever; read the most of the evening to him that he might sleep, and shall not soon forget it. When I reached the "Chateau," to add to my comfort, found that Miss Low had settled in her mind that C had the "varioloid" and excited the ladies with the idea of my bringing it to them in my clothes, which seemed to me supremely ridiculous, as Miss Platt had sent one case from her own ward and they knew I had attended poor Kenser for days. I told them if he were not better by to-morrow I would request of Dr. Bliss a room in the hospital, so as to save them from contagion. I retired to my room in disgust, taking care to shut the door, where I had a talk with Sister Southwick, with whom I can always exchange sentiments; wrote journal, indulged in a little home reverie to forget everything about me and was glad to fall asleep, though obliged to put on my bed all the clothes I could find to make myself comfortable.

December 8, 1863.

Was delighted to find C— out of bed and announced to the ladies at breakfast with pardonable satisfaction that he had recovered from the "smallpox"; wrote letter to Carrie to send with "Hospital Sketches" by Miss O. Dr. Smith called for them. After dinner— indisposed—went to bed, and for once was able to sleep, which I did until nearly dark. Spent the evening in my ward. Found Miss Felton, who went home a fortnight since to attend a wedding, at the "Home."

December 9, 1863.

Heartsick and anxious about No. 48, who has had three chills, a bad symptom after amputation; could not leave him while suffering, so could not go with Miss Platt to see Mrs. Dr. Jenkins—a pleasanter evening than the last, though could have no music, fearing to disturb 48. Found Sister S in her room waiting for me, and the Bostonians in "Officer" Low's room, having a nice little time with some sardines and olives and gingerbread—their usual style. Sister Griggs, who had been slighted also, came in and we had more fun over it than they did. I proposed rattling up our dishes for opposition, but afterwards concluded it would not be dignified for a "hospital sister." Retired at midnight.

December 10, 1863.

No. 48 passed the night without a chill, though he had a slight one this morning. Wrote from the ward master's book the names of my new patients in mine. Remained a while after dinner and opened the piano to forget myself in practising. Endeavored to put a few stitches in some things long waiting for them. Mrs. Jackson came in, with her unceasing flow of conversation. C came in just before five bringing the corkscrew, according to promise, so opened the grape wine, Sister Hill's present, which, with Sister Griggs's oatmeal crackers, we pronounced "splendid." Sisters Platt and Griggs joined us, and while we were endeavoring to get some warmth from our cheerful stovepipe, we heard Dr. Bliss's voice, bringing in some one to see the "Chateau." I arose to receive him and if he had looked toward the bottle of wine, etc., on the table, was ready to ask him to partake. Night was approaching, and her dusky veil covered our little festive scene, but we were quite ready with our parting salutations; went late to my supper, found Dr. Bliss had detained the ladies at the table, and was drilling them in "Rules and Orders." Was delighted to find two letters from home, when I returned to my ward, which "Danl." had put in a book to save for me, devoured them with a hungry spirit, which had been longing for something from the outer world. Indulged myself in looking over the dear home faces. Mrs. Jackson and Lieutenant Jacob's sister came in for a few moments, spent pleasant evening and promised to retire early, which after taking the rocking-chair by our pipe to warm before retiring I found rather difficult.

December 11, 1863.

In the evening went to Ward C to see Miss P— and C, happy at their "musical soiree." Miss Griggs and Dr. Robbins and I formed a most appreciative part of the audience, while reading an exceedingly interesting letter from Mrs. Ingersoll. The ladies were obliged to put on a variety of costumes for the night's rest, as we had no fire as yet, and my merino dressing gown over the other was just the thing.

December 12, 1863.

Dark and cloudy day. Wrote a line to the Chaplain of the Kalorama to hear from poor "Kenser." Spent the most of the day in the ward. Sister Southwick sent up her violinist to play for us, and I enjoyed it exceedingly without a crowd, sitting by my table writing to Sister G at the same time.

December 13, 1863.

Spent Sunday in my ward. Inspection late, so had my Special Diet to make out after dinner; remained awhile wondering if there were any religious services, when Sisters Platt and Griggs came in quite excited to know the reason why I was not present at the special meeting of the ladies at the "Chateau," where Dr. Bliss had been talking to them for an hour; found that "No. 6" had forgotten to give me the "Orderly's" message. Could not say I regretted it. Miss P insisted upon C and myself coming to Ward C to attend the services, which we did. The Senator from Maine addressed the meeting, in the absence of the chaplain. Mr.— as of old, came in for a few moments by the door. Services also in Ward E, where Sister Griggs accompanied the singing on our piano. Stumbled into a queer conversation; went to church with my new friend and relieved my conscience.

December 14, 1863.

Spent the most of the day in my ward, "No. 6" being out. Wrote letters. Quite a musical evening. The violinists and piano accompanying, tried to play myself, but was too nervous, and couldn't see the notes, but succeeded in pleasing the musical Irishman.

December 15, 1863.

Went to the Capitol for the first time since Congress met, and was, of course, exceedingly interested. Heard Senator Hale's indignant denial of the charge of political intrigue against the Senate and quite a spirited argument between the Senators from Maryland and

Kentucky. Mrs. Senator Lane came to see me, with Mr. Lovejoy. Am delighted to find she will be here this winter.

December 16, 1863.

No. 6 absent unaccountably and C took his place. Chaplain of Kalorama came to tell us that the men we sent there were doing well; wrote letter for "48" to his mother; he is decidedly failing, and had quite a satisfactory conversation with him. Mrs. Sheldon came to sing in the evening, and though I felt like sitting quietly by myself, put, as usual, myself out of the way and was only the nurse.

December 17, 1863.

My anxiety in part was relieved by seeing "No. 6" in the ward, whose report was more favorable than I anticipated. After dinner, which seemed quite homelike, was surprised to hear uncle J's voice in our little parlor, and delighted to see some one who could give me home news in detail. Concert in Ward A, which I could not attend.

December 18, 1863.

Packed a trunk to send by uncle J—, who came to see me, after dinner; went through the Smithsonian with him; attended lecture there in the evening, delivered by Rev. Mr. Lord, on "Civilization," with Sisters Griggs and Southwick and the delightful Dr. Banister, whom, however, I was glad to leave to the other ladies to entertain, as I was too weary to talk. Returned at nine to the "Chateau," where Miss Platt gave a little social entertainment from which no one of the sisterhood was excluded—New York affability. Retired immediately, glad for the hour for sleep. "No. 48" failing, wrote another letter to his mother. A new patient, found in the streets, strayed from a hospital.

December 19, 1863.

Spent part of the morning at the home while the ward was being cleaned. Went to the market, but finding no decent bread or cake, went to the bakery in spite of the cold. Was intending to return Mrs. Lane's visit, but the curtains were ready to be cut and devoted the afternoon to them. "No. 6" was out, so went to the house only for a few moments after giving out the medicine. In the evening a few of the men collected again and finished the curtains by eight, when I gave out the little lunch I had prepared for them, and as " Wood " came from Ward A with an urgent invitation for me to hear the violinists who were entertaining them, went up, found Dr. Banister and Miss Platt among the audience, Miss Griggs playing accompaniments, which she does beautifully, and C— and three others singing some new songs they had been practicing. The "Marseillaise" brought out Dr. Alcan, who sang it in French, much to our amusement, being more of a recitation than singing. Retired very late, which I regretted in the morning—weary, weary, weary; forgot I had devoted myself to suffering fellow-creatures, and was weak enough to long for a kind word for myself.

December 20, 1863.

Felt *miserably,* so went to church; decidedly wintry. Dr. Banister came home with me; after dinner went to my ward for a short time, procured a special pass for C— to witness the funeral ceremonies of Major-General Buford, then to the "Chateau" perfectly tired out. Went to bed and slept until dark; stupid evening with nothing particular to do but fret myself thinking of poor "48" whose hours are numbered. Ornamenting our ward, etc., etc., etc.

December 21, 1863.

Was surprised by an early visit from "Dahle," though C told me he was one of the escort of the remains of Major-General Buford. Commenced putting up curtains and preparations for Christmas and shall probably have no leisure until the day is over. " No. 48 " breathed his last about ten A.M., without a prayer or tear shed over him, though I know his poor mother will grieve when *she* hears the sad news. *Made wreaths* in the dining room after dinner and attended to Sister Southwick's comfort, who is quite ill. Ascertained that my poor *starved* man, found in the street, had a brother in the regiment now stationed here, procured a special "Pass," and sent a man after him, who soon returned with him and three others. Was agreeably surprised by a very *convenient* present from Sister S. The men did not feel like working at the wreaths, so postponed until the morrow. Was too weary to think of accompanying Sister G— and Dr. B— to Mr. Lord's lecture No. 2. Had a good practice, played over my old songs. Mrs. Ripley, from Concord, Mass. (with whom I have quite fallen in love), came in, and we had, as of late, a pleasant little *tete-a-tete—asked* me to sing "The long, long weary day" for her. Her husband died from fever contracted in the army, and she has come, hoping to soften her grief, by assisting in the work here.

December 22, 1863.

Made wreaths in dining room before dinner; ran away immediately after, to return Mrs. Lane's kind visit. Was delighted to receive a letter from Sister Gulie before I went; walked up and down the Avenue, searching in vain for a decent place where I could get some oysters, but was obliged to return hungry. "No. 6" had hung the rest of the curtains, which relieved my mind of part of the weight resting on it. The evergreens were brought in the ward after supper. Dr. Stuart came in to assist with his artistic taste and we made quite a happy commencement, as well as numbered twenty-two wreaths. Retired feeling weary only in body, refreshed in spirit.

December 23, 1863.

A pleasant day preparing for Christmas, as everything moved along very smoothly and am much pleased with the unique decorations of our ward which has received already so many compliments it quite puts one in good humor. Made poultice for C's wrist the last thing before coming home.

December 24, 1863.

Spent the entire day in my ward, busily trimming. Dr. Smith walked in just before dinner, invited me to take a drive, as the chaplain's horse needed exercise. Miss Jacobs accompanied us, and it was delightful. Saw the "Mountain Rangers" drilling their horses to leap a ditch, which amused us exceedingly. Made poultices for C, the sum total of my "nursing" to-day, excepting the usual round of duties. Received package of *Evening Posts*. Miss Platt received her box from Yonkers, in which was one for me from Mrs. Edward Martin, which delighted me, both because of the unexpected remembrance and of the pleasure of putting some nice, clean shirts under the pillows of my soldiers for Christmas. Mr. Ramsdell came in the evening with a friend; of course he was interested and admired the decorations. I was called to the ward-master's room, where I found Dr. S— with No. 6 *et al* making a "Santa Claus" —a medical one—which is fine, and prophesies a "Merry Christmas" tomorrow. Am thankful there is only *one* poor man in the ward who cannot enjoy it; and it cannot even disturb him, though he has, in my eyes, thrown a dark shadow on the picture all day. I arranged some presents for laundresses and others, and then retired, late as usual.

December 25, 1863.

I found my ward in the merriest mood, Dr. S— having already perpetrated a nice joke on Mrs. Wilson, whom he asked to prepare a little milk toast for an old man who had "come in the night and could eat very little"; she left her breakfast and prepared and took it in, and on inquiry for him her attention was directed to " Santa Claus," who is perched at the top of my post, with one leg over the beam, pack and hands filled, everything from the dispensary being purely medical, and the most complete thing of the kind I ever saw. The whole ward shouted with laughter, and she, perforce, with toast in hand, was obliged to join in the general merriment. No. 48's brother, who had come for his brother's remains, came in to see me. I was quite astonished and charmed with his unaffected simplicity, which enabled him to converse and thank me with a simple yet expressive brevity that was quite delightful. He said his mother wished him to come in and see me. Our ward was the center of attraction all day, and acknowledged by all—even by the "angel of Ward C"—to be the "banner ward" on this occasion.

I went to the "Chateau" after breakfast to make my Christmas toilet, and when I returned found a crowd (Mr. R among them) enjoying it immensely. The universal opinion was that our ward was dressed the prettiest, independent of our comical visitor; everyone admired the light border of evergreens, the holly vines on the ventilators, and the Christmas trees hung with bayonets, pistols, etc. Mr. Lovejoy went through the wards taking notes, so I suppose we shall soon see ourselves in print. I regretted to hear that our chaplain, Mr. Jackson, with Colonel Millett and Chaplain Adams of the Fifth Maine, had paid us a visit and was saluted with the cry of "Hay!" from all quarters, as he made such a fuss about their getting some of his hay by mistake to fill our merry patron saint, and when he ventured a joke and asked Sergeant Reed what they had given the old man for his breakfast, he answered him, "Hay," which he reported to the officer of the day, and Reed was obliged to go in to Dr. Bliss; but Dr. S— arranged things so, as he anticipated, he was allowed to go out for the first time and enjoy a Christmas dinner with some friends outside. The promised dinner of one hundred turkeys, etc., for the soldiers from Maine, was detained on the other side of the Schuylkill River, in consequence of the breaking of a bridge, with the rest of our Christmas boxes. I was delighted with a letter from Sister Gulie, informing me of the contents of my box, over which, good sister as she is, she had exerted herself to have it reach me to-day. At 6 P.M. we had religious services in "I." Chaplain Adams addressed us in a most beautiful and feeling manner, but was unfortunately interrupted by the ravings of a man who had been out making merry. Sisters Platt and Hill, with myself and some of the soldiers, formed the choir until C— came in and assisted with his tenor voice. Colonel Millett introduced me to the Rev. Mr. Adams, who was quite delightful, and Dr. Smith, who was also present with Colonel M, accompanied me to Ward E, which they said displayed the most beautiful taste of any they had seen. Walt Whitman and our French surgeon, Dr. Alcan, were most complimentary. Dr. S— asked me for some music and entertained us with a few songs. C was suffering from his wrist, and would not wait for them to leave, but made the poultice himself and went to "I" for his favorite diversion. Dr. Robbins came in soon after they left and said I had better go with him to " H " and hear the music, so concluded to keep Christmas merry as long as possible. I found Sister S— entertaining the gentlemen who had just left, and spent the rest of the evening there.

THE SHADOW AT CHRISTMAS

(From "The Drum Beat.")

During our preparations for Christmas, decorating the wards with evergreens, and making everything as bright as possible—for it is our duty to cheer and amuse the living as well as watch and attend to the sick and dying—there was one poor unfortunate boy, only eighteen, who, amid the unusual confusion and merriment, was to me, not yet quite callous to the sad contrasts we so often witness here, a strange shadow as he lay quietly, his life ebbing and flowing toward the great ocean of eternity. He had been found in the street, having, in a fit of delirium, strayed from his regiment, encamped in this vicinity. He had suffered from that fearful scourge, camp diarrhoea, for fifteen months, and being also a victim to intemperance, which might have been occasioned by his disease and privation, he presented such a picture of emaciation as I have never seen, except in the representations of the Libby prisoners. And yet from his manner of speaking, I could see that he had known what it was to be tenderly cared for, and, like the " prodigal son," penitent and sorrowing, was longing for that from which he had strayed. He held a small photograph of his mother firmly in one hand, as if that were all he had left to cherish. After two days he recovered a little strength, and, calling me to him, said, in a tearful, broken voice, " I wish my brother Benjamin was here, that I might put my two arms about his neck." I sent immediately to his regiment, and in a few hours his brother sat by his bedside, his full, rosy cheeks and bright eyes presenting a strong contrast to the wan face at which he gazed so sorrowfully, and from which suffering had so completely driven away all trace of youth that, although younger, he looked ten years his senior. He had been searching for him in street and hospital, and thinking he must have perished through exhaustion, had written that morning to his mother that they would probably never see him again. Like Benjamin of old, he was a great comfort, and when he left each day a hostage was demanded by his darling brother to insure his return—usually his pocket knife or comb—which he held in his hand to reassure him. At first his mind seemed laden with a heavy burden, and large tears would roll down his cheeks (or where they should have been). He told me he "was going to die, and wished some one would get him ready." I comprehended his desire to have some one tell him where to look for pardon and a guiding hand to lead him through the "dark valley," and brought one who often visits our hospital, and whom I believe to be one of the few faithful ministers of God among the soldiers, to his bedside, after which I had the great satisfaction of hearing him express himself much comforted. On Christmas Day the shadows of life seemed closing about him, and I feared the darker shadow of death would come like a specter to our Christmas feast; but he lingered at the threshold until the Sabbath, and the evening hour came before he found rest in that dreamless slumber whose reveille is only heard beyond the grave.

A. AKIN

Armory Square Hospital.

December 26, 1863.

Spent part of the morning at the "Chateau" sweeping our room, meditating, etc. Was detained in the ward by a constant succession of visitors, some very agreeable ones. In the evening I entertained myself with my own music, then went to Ward C for a short time, as I promised Miss S— to hear their new songs. When we returned Dr. S— read to us his written report of the "Hay" affair, which is capital.

No. 10, who is failing fast, though he has lived far beyond our expectations, was suffering and detained me a little after "Taps," and when I reached the home found a note from the officer of the day (Dr. Stearns) respectfully inviting the ladies to attend a "contraband wedding" [a wedding of freed slaves] in their new barracks just in the rear of our wards. All had retired but Sister Sand Mrs. I, who was spending the night here, so we all went together. We found there Drs. Stearns, Horsey, and Smith, and Colonel Millett, Miss Jacobs, Mrs. Wilson and family, and were in time to witness the ceremony, which was truly amusing. The bride and four bridesmaids wore thin white dresses and wreaths; one bridesmaid and groomsman carried a tall silver candlestick with candle. The bride shed tears very appropriately, but the bridesmaids giggled and one of their colored brethren, who had borrowed the chaplain's prayer book to read the service, made some amusing mistakes. We shook hands with the happy couple and left them enjoying the supper, which was very fine, roast turkey, etc., downstairs, and on another table upstairs three large frosted cakes, one ornamented very appropriately with an empty bird's nest. The supper occupied so much time we could not wait to witness the dancing. Dr. Stearns escorted me back to the house and I left Sister S— , who remained a while longer, hoping to see the dancing. I enjoyed the luxury of a pail of hot water, which with a lunch (being ravenously hungry) kept me up unusually late.

December 27, 1863.

To-day was rainy, and I was again obliged to defer going to Dr. Pyne's church. Mr. Webb came in from the dispensary and wanted me to go and see Dr. S—'s present, which had just arrived, and which is really very fine. I had a slice of the wedding cake, which I distributed in small pieces to some of the soldiers, much to their amusement. I found on going to dinner that Chaplain Adams was very much hurt by the ladies smiling during his remarks and was quite severe in his conversation with them when some of them went in to urge him to speak this afternoon, but at two o'clock he came in with the chaplain, and in his kind, fatherly way said it was all forgotten now. I did not feel equal to hearing Chaplain Jackson speak on religious subjects, though regretted to lose Mr. Adams's remarks, and being quite exhausted went to bed, and slept well, which was what I needed most just then. I found the brother of the poor man from Kuseville by his bedside, as I sent the ward master for him, feeling assured that he was dying; but he did not breathe his last until seven in the evening. Wrote in my journal until nearly nine, as I did not feel like joining in the singing, and went to the house early, when Sister Platt told me the result of her interview with Dr. Bliss, which quite pleased me, though remembered it would be *my turn* next. Mrs. Gray retires from her position in the "Special Diet Kitchen" to-morrow. Her departure means a great loss to the hospital.

December 28, 1863.

It is still raining. I spent the morning in the ward endeavoring to relieve and comfort my poor consumptive patient, who is the only particular one to care for now. There was never so little to do in the ward since I first came here, McDonald being the only one confined to his bed. I practiced a little, spent the afternoon at the house, and when I returned to the ward was greeted with the good news that my box had arrived. No. 6 had found it at the commissary's office and brought it in. After supper he wheeled it down, took off the top and brought it in, with his usual good sense and judgment, and a happy evening I have spent unpacking and lunching with my friends, Sisters Griggs and Southwick, and Dr. Banister, who came in to escort us to the lecture (which was postponed). Then I sent an invitation to C— and No. 6, and lastly to Sisters Platt and Hill. My heart is overflowing with love and thanks to my good Sister Guile, and indeed to all my sisters and friends who have so kindly interested themselves, and to-morrow I must write to them again.

December 29, 1863.

Beautiful weather. I spent the morning disposing of the contents of my delightful box and concluded to defer my tea party until to-morrow, having a headache. I went to Ward A to practice my duet with Sister Griggs, and before we finished, the Glee Club, with C at the head, came in and sang some new songs, which I enjoyed exceedingly, particularly the alto.

December 30, 1863.

Prepared for my entertainment, and put up my curtains, with the pink plaiting, which look fine. Took down my bed, made a lounge of the other, added a small table to the one from the parlor, and with Sister S's red table cloth, Carrie's frosted cake, Hattie's Santa Claus to preside, and all my nice eatables, the table looked quite to my satisfaction. My guests, seven in number, seemed to enjoy it vastly. Colonel Millett was my *vis-a-vis;* the others were Dr. Stuart with Sisters Griggs and Hill on either side and Sergeant Reed and Miss Platt. Miss Marsh, not being well, declined sitting down. The hot soda biscuits which Mrs. Jackson so kindly furnished were a mystery, in fact the ladies wondered how I could think of attempting such a thing as a tea company, but kindly pronounced it a "splendid success." Finding so much left, I arranged the table again, and sent for some of my soldiers to enjoy the feast also, which gave me the most pleasure. Dr. Banister came in to accompany the ladies to the lecture, which I was obliged to relinquish, and took a cup of coffee. Colonel Millett remained through the evening. After "Taps" the other ladies came in, and having kept the coffee and tea hot over our alcohol lamps, I invited them to partake of some. Misses Low and Felton, who could not sufficiently express their astonishment at my "getting up," enjoyed the pickles and dried beef, and after we had finished insisted upon helping me "wash up," which we did in great glee. Sister Hill did not leave until my bed was returned again to its proper place, for which I was thankful, being heartily tired, so much so that I could not go to sleep.

December 31, 1863.

Took luncheon at the house again from my "box" with Sister S— who was prevented from being with us last evening by one of her severe headaches. I returned dishes, etc., to Mrs. Jackson.

January 1, 1864.

I arose late to-day (a bad beginning for the new year), attended to a few patients in my ward, made some New Year presents of Fannie's handkerchiefs (which I had marked), and sent a present through the post office. Sisters Southwick and Griggs and myself were escorted by Dr. Banister to call upon the President. We were obliged to stand with the democratic crowd outside the gate until the dignitaries passed out, and were aggravated by a sight of their Napoleonic chapeaus, plumes, and gilded collars; then followed the army and navy officers on foot, the crowd meanwhile being permitted to press in. We succeeded in reaching the President's extended hand in safety, though at some risk, and were gratified with a view of Mrs. Lincoln in full "toilette," whom we thought exceedingly commonplace. We admired the blue room much, enjoyed the music, and were quite satisfied that we had paid our respects to the President on New Year Day.

Met Dr. Smith and Sister S—'s friend. The young and amiable Chaplain Hopkins with his sister was there. On our return found no dinner awaiting us, so invited Dr. B— to the "Chateau," and with Sister Grigg's box and my own, we were quite independent, but to our amusement, as well as their own, were interrupted by New Year visitors, the general ward master, Dr. Munger, and two of the hospital stewards. Dr. Smith and Colonel Millett called after I had left for the ward to take some tea and crackers to my poor consumptive patient, but took the trouble to come there and pay me a formal visit. There was singing in Ward C by some professors, acquaintances of Dr. Bliss, so the latter, with Mrs. B, Misses Lowell, Felton, and others were present. With a few exceptions, the singing was rather stilted, and our choir could have entertained better. Today the weather is extremely cold—quite a contrast to the delightful Christmas weather.

January 2, 1864.

I spent the morning in my ward, being anxious about my poor patient in bed No. 16, who suffers so much and is so patient and gentle. I cannot stay by him, and debated with myself whether I should sit by him or go to the home for a while. C said he would go down for his mince pie, so I concluded on the latter, and with Sister Southwick we spent an hour very pleasantly, but on returning to my ward was shocked and grieved to find the poor, suffering spirit I left there had passed away with scarcely a moment's warning. I refused to attend Mr. Lord's lecture, and went to the chaplain immediately after supper to see about sending a telegram to his brother in New York. I found Dr. Smith, with the rest of the family, seated about the table, and the doctor and Colonel M— very busily at work on the pretty frames made from cigar boxes. I then wrote a letter to his mother, which finished the evening.

January 3, 1864.

I intended to go to church, but it was so cold and found so much to detain me in my ward —C's wrist requiring more poulticing, and a new patient with a frightful-looking felon, and no attendant present for No. 4 (whose place No. 6 and I took *pro temps)*. I rushed to the home after dinner for a few moments, and back again as the services were to be held only in "E" and "K." A very interesting gentleman, just returned from a tour through the Holy Land, spoke to us from Job, and the men seemed more interested than usual; but to our astonishment, as well as disgust, the chaplain remarked, before commencing the services in "K," that they had been very much annoyed by loud talking in the other ward, which of course aroused our indignation, and immediately after the services were concluded I went to him (although C— was before me), and as publicly as possible asked an explanation, giving him at the same time our opinion that it was one of the most quiet and interesting services we had had in a long time. While delivering my lecture I was amused to see Mr. Lovejoy standing nearby enjoying it. There was appropriate music in Ward D in the evening, so went in for a short time, having promised sweet Mrs. Ripley to do so. Then I wrote letters for the dear ones at home, which I feel must go to-morrow.

January 4, 1864.

This day I shall long remember. Poor Mason's brother came in the night train as soon as he received the telegram, and he will take his body to New York this evening. Quite a heavy snowstorm is in progress.

January 5, 1864.

Spent the morning in my ward, anxious about Sergeant Reed, who has not been well since New Year Day. I felt miserable myself, but wrote for an hour after dinner, when I was obliged to go to our "home"; made a hot Sangaree, which I took and then went to bed, and when night came found I had too much fever to go out in the snow again, so made some tea and took it alone, Sister S— coming in to finish with me. Dr. B and some of the ladies went to the Smithsonian, but as the lecture was postponed, he returned and spent the evening with me. Miss P— and I read aloud from Buchanan Read's new poem, "The Wagoner of the Alleghanies." Misses Lowell and Felton dressed for an evening entertainment at Secretary Chase's, for the scientific professors now gathered here; Professor Agassiz came with them, which made my evening quite lively and interesting, though I rolled myself in my cloak and pillowed my head.

January 6, 1864.

Spent the day at the "Chateau," being quite ill. Sent a note to our surgeon in charge *pro temps* about the deluge. Received a letter from home, with sad news of dear Hattie's severe illness. C came down to inquire after my health and reported the condition of the ward, etc. After tea went to the ward a few moments, and to Ward F to hear the gentleman (Dr. Diehl, our consul to Java), who spoke to us on Sunday, tell of his travels in the Holy Land. He is exceedingly interesting. The Boston trio came in at "Taps" from the scientific tea party in the "Special Diet Kitchen," and bringing some tea and coffee, we partook of some before retiring.

January 7, 1864.

I awoke early with the sound of falling waters still in our ears and found we had no fire and that Uncle Ben was unable to get to the furnace in consequence of the flooding. I succeeded in keeping myself from perishing by the alcohol lamp, over which (for my breakfast) I made a cup of tea, to drink with my cold toast spread with jelly, and heated water to put in a bottle, with which I warmed my benumbed fingers. I managed to get dressed by ten. I had the pleasure of meeting Mr. Lord, our fine Smithsonian lecturer, before I left the house, and after the contrabands had baled us out and our fire was started. Called at the chaplain's to return some dishes and inquire after the invalids. It is decided the Colonel has *not* the smallpox. Went to my ward, found "Reed" better, read to him the first number of our *Hospital Gazette,* of which Mrs. Ingersoll is editor, and which is printed by two patients. Two new patients from Company K arrived. Our interesting lecturer again came to Ward F and entertained us for an hour delightfully. Dr. Robbins called at the "Chateau" after "Taps" and spent an hour.

January 8, 1864.

More snow fell, which did not improve our walking. Wrote letter to Clara Okell. No letter from home yet, and I pray our dear little

Hattie may be recovering. Remained in my ward until late in the afternoon as No. 6 went out. Went to Dr. Bliss's office to get an order for cranberries signed, as I was fully determined to try that poultice for No. 17. Spent evening in Ward C, where the "Glee Club" entertained us with music, and Miss Platt's friend, Miss Torrey of New York, came over from Professor Henry's at the Smithsonian, where she is staying.

January 9, 1864.

Spent the morning in the ward and after at the house. Shared Sister G—'s indignation about the punch order and enjoyed the finale. Miss Thomas came and sang while I was absent. Our lecturer came again in the evening for the third time. I did not enjoy his lengthened remarks about women, and being chilled and tired left before he finished. Sister G— gave us some "Noyeau" and I produced some cake, which soon brought us to a more delightful state, and inclined me to retire early.

January 10, 1864. Found No. 17 had been suffering severely, seemingly from erysipelas in his wound, the same as Sergeant Reed and McDonald, which is strange. No. 49 not any better. Did not leave my ward until dinner hour. Inspection is losing some of its disagreeable features, as we are always marked "perfect." Dr. Bliss was pleased to pause and admire the picture from home which is now on my table. Took coffee and cake at the "Chateau" after dinner. Attended service in Ward F, and was charmed by the remarks of the Rev. Mr. Ecclestone, from Newark, N.J., but was disgusted by our chaplain's inviting [Senator "Jim" Lane from Kansas](#) to speak again (as he had already once done so in "D") on the slavery question, as I wished so much the impressive remarks of the former might long remain in the memories of the soldiers; and as I think Sunday is no fitting day for the discussion of that question by such an unprincipled man as he is supposed to be, I made my escape as soon as possible. After supper I read to Leech (No. 17) from Hood to divert his mind, until it was time to go to church. Accompanied Sisters Hill, Platt, Marsh, and Southwick to Dr. Sunderland's, who preached the funeral sermon of Elisha Whittlesy, who married a

Miss Mygatt, of New Milford, Conn., and dead nearly a year since. It was a fine sermon. Mr. Robbins and family were there, and father and son insisted upon escorting us home.

January 11, 1864.

No. 49 is improving; the others are about the same. I left them in No. 6's care, and accompanied Sisters Griggs and Southwick to the Capitol, as we heard the Rev. Mr. Ecclestone would open the Senate proceedings. Received a long letter from Sister Mary saying Hattie was better, so with a grateful heart was ready to enjoy almost anything. For some unknown reason Dr. Sunderland made the opening prayer instead of Mr. E—, and we were interested in the remarks about Garrett Davis's expulsion from the Senate, despite the fact that the resolution was laid over, and after the announcement of the death of one of the senators from West Virginia and eulogies spoken, the Senate adjourned. Met Dr. Robbins and Mrs. Senator Lane of Indiana on our way to the House. I introduced myself to her, thus saving the time for calling at the hotel, and found her very cordial and pleasant as I remembered her, though time had marked some lines on her face. Remained but a short time in the House as it was preparing to adjourn also, and *we*

> "Began to feel, as well we might,
>
> The keen demands of appetite."

Sister G— left us at 4-1/2 Street to dine with a friend, and when Dr. R— left us at Seventh Street Sister S— and I went in search of oysters, but failed to find any, so contented ourselves with fresh rolls, which we brought home and with the other good things we had in our room and a cup of coffee, made quite a dinner. As I was utterly worn out I was obliged to take a rest. Our lecturer came for the fourth time in Ward D; as No. 6 was going out and my head still weary, I did not care to have it in "E." Instead of going to the lecture for which I had no heart I wrote a note to Mrs. Martin, to acknowledge her kind remembrance of me. Miss Chapin, a friend of Sister G— (both accomplished and beautiful), came to pass the night with her. The former failing to find a place here, as she was promised, is on the staff of a hospital in Baltimore, of which Dr. B's brother is the head. Some ladies and gentlemen had called on Miss Platt and myself, and found the card of Mrs. Cleveland of Yonkers. Miss Felton is having a grand time with the professors, and in company with Professor Agassiz she has the *entrée* to all the entertainments given to them, which is the last thing on the carpet of society at present. To-day Miss Felton went with a large party to Arlington, General Robert E. Lee's old home.

January 12, 1864.

My patients are all improving excepting Sergeant Reed, who is still suffering from chills. I was astonished to see No. 23 of last summer, just returned from his long furlough, looking so well. Father Duffy, formerly our old attendant, surprised us, too, with a call which was highly amusing, saying, as he grasped my hand, "Bless me, how glad I am to see you!" and for ten minutes (which seemed much longer) overwhelmed me with his Irish blarney and volubility; then he insisted upon my playing the "Irish Washerwoman" for him.

As No. 6 went out, C— took his place, but I had only reached our "Home" when he came to bring me a dear, good letter from Sister Carrie. In the evening, after attending to my patients, I went to the Smithsonian with Sister Griggs, whose society I enjoy vastly, to hear one of Professor Agassiz's scientific lectures on "The Glaciers." Our soldiers had the privilege of a pass from the officer of the day to attend it also.

January 13, 1864.

Found my patients improving, so concluded to go again to the Senate chamber and hear the great debate about the expulsion of Garrett Davis, and we sat there from twelve to past four. Davis spoke three hours and poured out his vials of wrath and torrent of abuse on Senator Wilson of Massachusetts, who offered the resolution to expel him, which at first was at least entertaining, but at the last became so spiteful and disgusting. Senator Wilson replied in a half hour's speech, and although a man of quite ordinary talent, he was too evidently on the right side to admit of but one opinion. The debate will be continued and I hope will end in Davis's expulsion, not only for proposing to have the people take the affairs of government in their own hands and change the administration, but because, from his irascible nature and uncontrolled passions, he is not fitted for a seat in our Senate. I was glad to go to supper, having had no dinner. Wrote a long letter home in the evening, although weary and worn out.

January 14, 1864.

The Christmas dinner has at last arrived, and the "turkey-birdies," which have given occasion for so much talk and rhyme, have been properly taken care of. Mrs. Hannibal Hamlin (to honor the gift, being from Maine) came through the hospital at dinner time. Mrs. Ingersoll introduced her to me, and her husband's daughter, a sweet-looking young lady. She was very pleasant and affable. In the evening Vice President Hamlin, with others, came to Ward K, and made short speeches. "*America*" was sung by our "Glee Club."

January 15, 1864.

To-day was cloudy and the walking bad. Spent most of the day in the ward. Succeeded in writing a note of thanks to cousin Lydia Thorne, who so kindly contributed to my box. Yesterday being pay day, many of the men went out to-day, and thinking the others seemed lonely, invited the soldier violinist to come and play for us. Practiced and wrote in the evening, took a box of guava jelly to the youthful-looking Philadelphian in "D," Mrs. Ripley's ward.

January 16, 1864.

The following event attended by our author was historic. Young Anna Dickinson was a pro-war Quaker and the first woman to ever address the U.S. House of Representatives. She was an anti-slavery activist, feminist, friend to Susan B. Anthony, and at only 19 years old, delivered a well-received speech to 5,000 listeners at Cooper Institute in New York.—Ed. 2014

Went with Miss Griggs and Corporal Hartshorne, who is transferred from Ward C to be her ward master, to hear Anna Dickinson's address in the House of Representatives, and returned proud that such talent should have been given to a woman. Her delivery is wonderful, and seems more the effect of inspiration than the power of intellect. Her "Words of an Hour" were on the theme in which our hearts are now most deeply interested, "The War." Her graphic pictures could not fail to bring unbidden tears to the eyes of many of her attentive listeners, and her final appeal to the patriotism of the young men was supremely eloquent; even a synopsis of her lecture would fail of conveying the power of her thrilling language or the effect of her fine intonation. Dr. Robbins came in with Miss Marsh, having been her escort, and we were quite lively with our enthusiastic descriptions to Miss Platt, interspersed with a slight skirmish with Mrs. Ingersoll about the "Woman's Rights" question, which quite delighted Mrs. R— and Misses F— and Sister G— treated us in her room to a glass of "Noyeau" [Crème de Noyeau is an almond flavored cordial syrup] to revive our exhausted powers, which I hoped would bring immediate sleep.

January 17, 1864.

Spent the morning in the ward, but could not oblige myself to remain after dinner. Had a "rollicking" conversation with Misses Low, Hill, and Felton about the former's pet cat, which we proposed poor "Uncle Ben" should hang the next morning, and finished the evening by writing an amusing account of the religious (!) services in Ward B, to be submitted to Dr. Bliss for the *Hospital Gazette,* and taking a cup of tea with Misses Low and Felton, sitting on the floor in their room. Retired late of course.

(For the Hospital Gazette.)

Religious (?) services were conducted in some of the wards very much as usual. The speaker in Ward "B" being some one interested in the Ohio Relief Society, whether citizen or layman we cannot report, he informed us that he was satisfied the agents had failed in doing their duty and the Ohio soldiers had been neglected by them, when he took his seat much to the satisfaction of his audience. Our chaplain (Mr. Jackson, from Maine) then arose and said he had been interested in the remarks of this good man from Ohio, who represented the church and bar of the northern part of Ohio, and he had had occasion to observe that the Ohio men had been neglected by the Representatives of that State, and that things sometimes went astray; but it was consoling to know that though the things intended for the soldiers did not reach them, their families were visited and cared for by the people at home, for which they ought to be very grateful, and the goodness of God leadeth to repentance, after which came the benediction.

January 18, 1864.

To-day was a rainy day. The ward was unusually quiet. C has left to be captain of the laundry. Natze has passed his last examination for discharge, and his bewhiskered face will not much longer present an evening picture to arrest the attention of the ladies passing through. Sergeant Reed's brother and sister have arrived and hope to take him home with them. Two old patients from furlough have returned. Another canary bird (which proves to be a singer) graces the opposite window, a present from one of the men to Dr. Stuart's ward, which we name "Tommy."

January 19, 1864. Mrs. Abby Gibbons, the philanthropist, visited our hospital in company with others, and had the pleasure of a few moments' conversation with her, and also with the Rev. Mr. Storrs, of Brooklyn, who was brought to my ward by Dr. Smith, and, as I always supposed, is charming in conversation. He asked me to furnish him with some of the many interesting incidents of our hospital life for a paper which he intends to publish during the sanitary fair. I gave him my sister's address in Brooklyn. After dinner, feeling altogether weak and miserable, I went out for fresh air and to find a piano tuner. Called at the Sanitary Commission on Dr. Jenkins, of Yonkers, who is in town, but did not find him. I then went with a party from the hospital to hear Mr. Gough lecture on "Temperance," and was glad to see that the crowd was immense and exceedingly interested and impressed. Made cup of tea, and Sister G— furnished us with some nice cake.

January 20, 1864. A new patient with face swollen frightfully with erysipelas arrived. Copied the names of those who contributed to Dr. Stuart's present. Had a very satisfactory conversation with Dr. Babcock, the New York medical agent. Arranged the ward for the evening and wrote invitations to Dr. Bliss and others to be present at the presentation to Dr. Stuart. Our ward was filled at 7 P.M. and everything but the last speech from one of the Representatives was as it should be, and as our friends are pleased to say, a "success." The band of music was fine, and as soon as C— brought in Dr. S— played the opening piece; then Mr. Perley, of Erie (Dr. Stuart's home) made the presentation speech, while I brought out the box of valuable instruments from my medicine chest at the proper moment. Dr. S— commenced his reply very feelingly and fittingly, but modesty and nervousness prevented him from finishing; then we had "Rally Round the Flag, Boys," from our " Glee Club," and an excellent speech from Dr. Bliss, music from the band, speeches from Hon. Judge Schofield, of Erie, Pa., and Hon. Amos Meyers, and music until "Taps." The ward was crowded, surgeons and all honoring us with their presence. Misses Low and Felton entertained us at the "Chateau," where we found Dr. Stearns also, with tea and cake, which, with the excitement of the evening, kept me awake half of the night.

January 21, 1864.

I was delighted to have the opportunity of driving and of breathing the fresh air and accepted instantly Miss Platt's invitation to make one of a party to Fort Corcoran, with Sisters Griggs and Southwick and Lieutenant-Colonel Millett. We found the house which Colonel Tannatt made his headquarters burned, and nothing but a pile of bricks left to tell the sad tale; and at Colonel Whistler's they were afflicted with varioloid, so proceeded to Fort Cass, where we made a pleasant call on Mrs. Tannatt, and thence to the Arlington House, which I had so long desired. I was of course exceedingly interested, and brought away some ivy and rose buds, as the shrubs were in leaf, as relics; we were forbidden access to the "attic." We took our lunch in the ambulance, a part of which Miss G— and I could not resist sharing with some soldiers, who were resting by the wayside. We reached home by three, and noticed that all the public buildings were draped with black to honor the memory of the senator from Virginia.

January 22, 1864.

Sergeant Reed left for home with his brother and sister, and to my great surprise McDonald received a transfer to General Hospital, Boston, and was taken away at a few hours' notice, his bed put on a stretcher and in an ambulance which took him to the train; the latter had a hospital car, fitted for the accommodation of such patients. Fearing the ward would feel melancholy over the loss of two who had been so conspicuous, I invited Misses Griggs and Platt and the "Glee Club," and we had quite a musical and pleasant evening, commencing with our duet. When we had finished I went to Ward H, where some of the men were trying to dance, the music of the violin being irresistible. Wrote a letter to Jobes. We are having beautiful spring weather.

January 23, 1864.

As it is a splendid day I insisted upon having our ward thoroughly cleaned, beds taken out and aired, etc. I invited two of my old wounded patients to our "home," fearing they might take cold, and entertained them for an hour or two. Mrs. Senator Lane and two young ladies called and they were extremely pleasant and sociable. They invited me to accompany them to one of Speaker Colfax's receptions next Friday evening. "Nourlinger," another of last summer's patients, left to-day on furlough. Miss Francis (niece of Lydia Maria Child) arrived last night to take Miss Fe]-ton's place, who leaves on Monday. Enjoyed a good practice in my own ward and some good music in Ward A. Sister Griggs and a friend who brought in his flute gave us some very nice duets.

January 24, 1864.

Being a fine spring day to-day, Sister Griggs and I took advantage of it and went to Dr. Pyne's church. I was [159] quite interested in the venerable structure, etc., but returned very much fatigued, the walk being over two miles, and having partaken of a very light breakfast indulged myself in a refreshing sleep after dinner, finding myself sufficiently exhausted in body to be able to do so, though regretted to lose Dr. Sunderland's address, who was invited to assist in our religious services to-day. Wrote a letter to Sister Cornelia. Went to Ward I with Miss Platt, as the " Glee Club " were expected to sing, it being Miss Felton's last evening here, where we found Professor Henry and lady; but they sang only a short time, being invited to sing in the Baptist church by Mrs. Green, who assists us so often with her alto. At "Taps" we gathered in the parlor of our "Chateau" in honor of Miss Felton's departure. Partook of coffee, cake, etc., and made as much noise as ten ladies could conveniently without any tin pans or broomsticks. Valedictory speeches abounded, and having found that one had retired quietly, declining to be present, she was immediately brought before the appreciative audience assembled in the broad hall, in a very compulsory manner, after which we retired, quite satisfied by the fact that "there is no Sunday in the Army."

After retiring I improvised for the amusement of the other ladies who were disrobing,

A DIRECTORY FOR THE "LADIES' CHATEAU"

Sisters Southwick and Akin
Have Room No. 1,
Who keep smoked beef and pickles
And plenty of fun.
In Room No. 2
Are olives and figs,
Beside the fair inmates—
Sister Platt and our Griggs.
In Room No. 3
You will find if you please,
Our dear Sister Hill
And her wonderful "sneeze."
With her, Sister Marsh Is obliged to abide,
Who complains that the talking
Is all on her side.
Next; sweet Mrs. Ripley,
With "Bangor" to boot,
Which means though so quiet
Some things do not suit.
On the opposite side
You'll find Felton & Co.; And if not tea-drinking
Don't blame Sister Low.
And last, though not least,

> In the "Home of the Nurses, Misses Lowell and Francis—
> So here end my verses.

Made a copy of the verses for memento of Sister Felton's last evening, and gave them to her inscribed, for

> Our dear Sister Felton,
> So good and so wise,
> Yet withal is so gleeful,
> She laughs with both eyes.

January 25, 1864.

An agreeable visitor in the evening, with whom I had not enjoyed a conversation in a long time, and felt much better for it; left my ward at eight, as he wished to accompany me to our "Chateau," and we *finished* our talk before the cheerful stove pipe. Colonel Wysewell, who had charge of the invalid corps here, also made me a short call immediately after supper.

January 26, 1864.

Our splendid weather continues; spent the morning preparing for inspection by the Surgeon General, who passed through with Dr. Bliss and others about twelve, with one hurried glance, while I was resting quite wearied out. At sunset put on a bonnet and went to call on Colonel who sustains my good opinion, and who promised to use his influence for something better than that for which I asked, which so delighted me that I was obliged to walk through Smithsonian grounds to allow the exuberance of spirits to subside. C came in the evening, and when I told him of it he could scarcely credit it. Mr. Ramsdell made quite a visit and interrupted my letter writing, so was obliged to keep very late hours, to finish my talk to Sister Gulie, as I was determined the letter should not be delayed.

January 27, 1864.

This was a fine morning. I went with C to Colonel W's office and waited a half-hour before he came in; then in his usual pleasant way he gave him directions how to proceed, though the desired haven seemed more distant than we wished. Walked home and rested a while in our little parlor.

January 28, 1864.

The fine weather tempted me out of doors again, although my head was a little troublesome. Accompanied Sisters Southwick and Griggs and Dr. Banister to the Capitol, where we found the Senate again discussing Mr. Wilson's resolution about Garrett Davis, but as the air was so stifling, and

Mr. W not at all brilliant, left feeling more need of rest than of anything else. Called at the National Hotel to see Mrs. Lane a moment. Sister Hill gave me a glass of delightful wine, and I was glad to rest until tea time.

January 29, 1864.

We concluded to improve the fine spring weather and have our "Chateau" cleaned, so Uncle Ben and Aunt Sally commenced immediately after breakfast. Patterson (No. 6) came and took up my matting, and after dinner he put it down in the very best manner, and assisted me in putting things in order, Sister Southwick having gone out for a drive. Johnny (my drummer) came, too, and waited upon me. Hon. Mrs. Lovejoy called to see us and brought his niece with him. Went to see Dr. Banister to request of him the favor to have a friend of No. 17 transferred to our ward, which he kindly granted, and to Ward D to say goodby to C—'s friend, who left today, having received his furlough. Went again to see Mrs. Lane and engaged to go with them to Speaker Colfax's reception; then to the florist's, and found a japonica and some fine white flowers, which Miss Platt arranged very prettily in my hair. C— came at eight, when my toilette was pronounced completed and I was "showed up" to the few ladies remaining at home (the most of them having gone to the Campbell Hospital entertainment), who kindly escorted me to the hotel where I found Mrs. Lane awaiting, and also Major Mace and Dr. Fry, who was my escort, and whom I found more than usually interesting, he having charge of all the hospitals in Kentucky and Indiana. The reception was crowded. I was introduced to some one every other moment, and had the pleasure of a conversation with Judge Holt, of Kentucky, whose fine face was an index of his character. Mrs. and Miss C, a sister of the Speaker, received

Secretary Crittenden, our Vice-President, lady and daughter, and Major Generals Doubleday and Schenck were among the guests. Met Dr. Stearns and Mr. and Mrs. Robbins also. I was amused to meet the Rev. John Pierrepont, of Boston, and his last wife, of whose romantic marriage I had heard. Took coffee and went to the basement, from which issued feeble sounds of music. I succeeded in obtaining a slight view of some slightly animated figures moving about in a hollow square. Had the company of Senator Lane and Major Mace to the gate and found the rest of the ladies waiting to comment on the hospital nurse's toilette and hear what she had seen and heard. The major invited me, with Mrs. Lane, to attend the matinee at the White House the next day.

January 30, 1864.

Today was cloudy. Took my breakfast in bed, which seemed quite homelike, and dressed at my leisure. Went to my ward, attended to special diet, and left all things in charge of my faithful Patterson again. Spent three hours delightfully in driving and making visits, first at the White House, where we found so few people that we had a fine opportunity of observing the President and his lady, with whom Mrs. Lane conversed while I was pretending to do the same with a Scotch gentleman, Mr. McCloud, whom I met the evening before. I went to the conservatory and made our adieus. Left a card at Lord Lyons'; called on Mrs. General Canby, whose husband is now Assistant Adjutant General at the War Department. Was quite weary in the evening, but was entertained by a German in our ward whom we have found to be quite a musician; although he has not practiced in twenty years, his renderings of some sweet German waltzes was keenly enjoyed. Sisters Griggs and Platt came in, too, and C— returned from the Sanitary Fair; the former played her dreamy waltzes before we left for "Home."

January 31, 1864.

Inspection very late. Studied tactics with C— in his new book after dinner a while preparatory for examination, and also diligently scanned a map which Miss Hill kindly lent us. Then attended services in wards A and K, where we listened to some very good remarks from a Representative from Iowa, which we were glad to accept in our spiritually starved state. The music from our hospital choir was appreciated in Ward K. Went with Sister Griggs to speak to Colonel Harris and Captain Russel, who are still there, both very pleasant gentlemen, the latter particularly so. We were exceedingly gratified in the evening by having the Episcopal evening church service read by the Rev. Mr. Parvin, of Ohio, who also addressed us in a most impressive manner. The Rev. Dr. Munger added a short but very affecting sermon. Both of these clergymen are engaged in the work of the Christian Commission. Our soldiers were unusually impressed, and many of them said they could have listened all night. They paid the most profound attention, and when we saw how gratefully the words of our impressive church service were received into their weary, saddened, thirsting hearts, we said it is not true that the rough soldier's heart is steeled against spiritual influence, and it is only when sermons are meted out to them in "rations" with a sparing hand and a cold heart that they fail in rousing their better nature and are made subjects of ridicule. For our own part we felt strengthened and lifted from the depressing influences about us and grateful that we had witnessed such proof of the power of our beautiful service. We had the pleasure of shaking hands with them, and received an invitation to attend the anniversary of the Christian Commission at the House of Representatives on Tuesday evening. Sister Platt was brought down to the "Home" faint and quite ill.

February 1, 1864.

Our hospital received over one hundred patients and our ward fifteen (betokening a move on the part of the Army of the Potomac), none of them very ill, but making a long medicine list. Sweet Mrs. Ripley is quite ill and I have promised to make out her diet tomorrow. I went to Ward C to hear the "Glee Club," assisted by Mrs. Greene; practiced for the dedication of the new chapel, although feeling quite ill, and after reaching the "Home" in desperation took a cup of tea from Miss Low, and some of Miss Lowell's ginger cakes, which she urged me to accept.

February 2, 1864.

Passed a miserable night, did not sleep until after midnight, and have spent most of the day in bed. Received a good, long letter from Gulie, and a little one from Hattie, which I enjoyed to the utmost, and which almost made me forget my indisposition. Mrs. Ripley came and spent an hour with me, reading poetry, etc., very pleasantly. We have had quite a hospital at our "Chateau," as Mrs. Ingersoll is still here, we now number four, and excepting Mrs. Ingersoll, none of us required the aid of a surgeon, which we hear is considered very independent and commendable on our part. Was disappointed in not being able to go with the party to the anniversary of the Christian Commission. Sister Griggs was also obliged to remain, to play for our "choir," which is to practice for the first time in the new chapel.

February 3, 1864.

Took breakfast at the "Chateau" but went to my ward soon after and devoted myself to it. I was rejoiced to see "Kensor" return quite recovered from smallpox, though his face shows still very plainly the marks of that dreadful disease. Received a present of a fine gold pen and handle in morocco case from a young soldier who has only been a week in the ward; he tempted me into a conversation at first by handing me two apples, which like Mother Eve I did not refuse, so he gained courage to make this presentation. Went to the chapel on our grounds (which is just finished) to hear our choir practice with Mrs. Green and Miss Billings, a soprano whom C— was pleased to be obliged to go for, with Mrs. G— in the ambulance. Dr. Bliss came in, and made some happy suggestions to the leading tenor, which caused the benignant smile to pass from his countenance and gave him altogether the appearance of a rooster caught in a summer shower. Wrote in journal in the evening, while C sat by the desk and dispatched two letters in his usual desperate style; then studied tactics and formed "platoons" with my new pen and handle.

February 4, 1864

As Dr. Stuart was quite ill, and after waiting until nearly twelve, I made the rounds myself, prescribed diet, etc., which amused my patients much. Our chapel was dedicated this afternoon. Rev. Dr.

Marks (author of "The Peninsular Campaign") preached the sermon and our choir sang the anthem, etc., beautifully. The church was filled, and altogether it was quite an interesting occasion. I played over my music before quite an audience of new patients. Sister Marsh entertained us at the house with mince pie, cake, and tea, having received a box, and Sister Southwick's apples have arrived.

February 5, 1864.

Found no surgeon in my ward, and also Charlie M with the measles, rapidly developing as we supposed. Reported to the officer of the day, and had three in half an hour. Dr. Horsey made the rounds. Bound my carpet rug. Felt the need of exercise so much that I took a walk with Sisters Hill and Griggs. Called on Messrs. Blanchard and Graham, our fellow-passengers on the *James S. Green,* when we went to New York last September, a five days' sail from Washington never to be forgotten, but they were both out, and on our return called at the chaplain's to see Lieutenant Colonel Millett, who is quite ill again and complains of the ladies being unsociable; but No. 6 soon came to tell me Miss Thomas was in the ward, and found the friend with her was Miss Robinson (Dr. Bowen's friend). She gave us some very fine instrumental music, and Miss T sang, which of course soon attracted many visitors. C— came in, and in his enthusiastic manner showed me the second letter from his regiment, which was a recommendation for promotion, that was all one could wish, and in which I fully sympathized. Charlie was suffering severely with his throat, but Dr. Munger (who has charge of us now until Dr. S— recovers) was attending to him. Harris presented me with a set of dice of his own manufacture. While feeding Charlie something which I had prepared soft for his supper, Sister S— sent an invitation to accompany her to George William Curtis's lecture, which, although completely tired out, I could not refuse. I am delighted that I did not, for I enjoyed it beyond anything I have heard yet. His "Way of Peace" is a sad and sorrowful way, but seems the only sure one. He was a little unjust to Governor Seymour and he places the Abolitionists a little too high on the record of events, but altogether it was a good lecture, and gave me a better knowledge of myself. Dr. Banister, who accompanied us with Sister Griggs, is a stanch Democrat, and we told him he looked like "a sadder and a wiser man."

February 6, 1864.

Dr. Munger made early rounds but was glad to see Dr. S— come in later as I am so worried about Charlie M—, thinking he may possibly have the smallpox. A number of patients were brought in from a sad railway accident at the "Long Bridge," [a bridge built in 1809 upstream from Georgetown] three from our ward, who fortunately were not much injured. In the evening, while Curtis and Cross gave us some music with the violin and piano, I wrote an account of the Episcopal service we enjoyed last Sabbath evening, for *Hospital Gazette,* and played backgammon with No. 6.

February 7, 1864.

Dr. Butler died two days ago, and his funeral service was held today.

The chaplain had a short service in our chapel, and it was homelike and pleasant to see people going to church and particularly gratifying to see the soldiers, with limbs and without limbs, gathering to a house of prayer. Some of us did not enjoy the evening service, which was a Methodist prayer meeting, though I was interested to hear three or four of the men express their religious convictions with much seeming sincerity. We ladies concluded, after we reached the "Chateau" and expressed our feelings, that we should petition for a regular service once on Sunday, and then took a little "Noyeau" to strengthen our resolution as well as ourselves, after the long "sitting."

February 8, 1864.

As Mrs. Ripley's cold is worse, I made out her requisition for diet. Some new patients arrived from "Convalescent Camp," which is broken up. Took luncheon at the house in place of dinner with Mrs. Rand, Miss Low; went with Sister G to the temperance meeting at the chapel in the evening, intending to stay but a short time, but did not like to disturb the crowd; however, when Chaplain Jackson "ventured to make a remark," with C's assistance I made my way out. Went to the dispensary for medicine for Mrs. R which I had promised her; found Dr. Stuart and Mr. Ramsdell, with whom I had quite a chat, while Mr. Webb was preparing the medicine. Sister S— had kept the tea hot for me, the rolls, etc., in readiness, to which I intended to return much earlier.

February 9, 1864.

George William Curtis repeated his fine lecture, entitled "The Way of Peace," in our little chapel, which I am sure must do a world of good, apart from the present enjoyment, in which soldiers and all seemed to participate. Afterwards spent an hour with Mrs.—, who is still ill. Had a severe headache in the evening. Read Dickens's Christmas story, "Mrs. Lirriper's Lodgings," while C wrote his application to the Provost Marshal. Messrs. Oilman and Blanchard, fellow-passengers on the *James S. Green,* paid us a visit, accompanied by a gentleman, Mr. Bull, and Mr. B sent us some copybooks.

February 10, 1864.

No surgeon again; Dr. S— ill in bed. No. 4, attendant, came in after an absence of two days, ill with erysipelas. I prescribed the famous cranberry poultice and went with my Extra Diet to Dr. Bliss, with whom I had a long conversation about the two most absorbing topics to us ladies at present—Mrs. I— and the chaplain, in which the ladies were so much interested that I was obliged to have an audience at the "Chateau" after dinner. Took tea with Sister S— , then after giving out Special Diet I went with Dr. Banister and Sister Griggs to hear the Rev. Pierrepont* deliver his poem on "Fashion." I was heartily disgusted and indignant over his reading of the poem, as there was neither wit nor sense to excuse his vulgarity, and coming from a clergyman who has reached the venerable age of threescore and ten, it was in the extreme disgusting and his blaspheming painful. The only apology his friends can make for him is that he is in his dotage. Drs. Robbins and Stearns took tea and cake with us at the "Chateau." There is a large fire on the avenue, reported to be the President's stable.

*Undoubtedly John Pierrepont, abolitionist, Unitarian minister, and poet.—Ed. 2014

February 11, 1864.

Accompanied Sisters Griggs and Southwick to Georgetown to call upon Captain Russel (late of Ward K), who is a New Yorker from Salem, Washington County, near Saratoga. He amused me with his misanthropical remarks, evidently caused by some sad disappointment. Called on Mrs. Senator Lane also. Denied myself the pleasure of going to Ward F, where our music was congregated, and wrote letters.

February 12, 1864.

Dr. Kennon sent to our ward, as Dr. S, at my suggestion, reported himself off duty. Miss Low announced Miss Felton's engagement to Mr. Ledyard, a relative of Governor Seymour.

February 13, 1864.

Received a charming note from Rev. Dr. Storrs, and commenced a piece for his little paper, the *Drum Beat*. Was delighted to have inspection this afternoon, instead of to-morrow, it being more than what we had hoped.

February 14, 1864.

Mr. Murdoch read in our chapel from the Scriptures and some most effective pieces of sacred poetry in his magnificent style. A genuine March day. Went to Trinity, corner C and Third Streets, to-day being the first Sunday in Lent, and heard a very good sermon explaining this custom in the church. Met the Wilsons, who invited me to take a seat in their pew.

February 15, 1864.

Wrote valentines to Sisters Hill and Southwick, who were indisposed at the "Chateau." After dinner went to Dr. Bliss's office to ask for certificate for C; met Dr. Stuart in dispensary, looking miserably; he requested of me one of my *carte de visites*. I concluded he was getting childish, or that he was thinking of leaving us. Went to Ward A to enjoy a little music with Sister

Griggs; Sister P— followed, and after playing our duet C— came to see if we were going to Ward K according to invitation; but the slight snow having prevented Mrs. Green from coming, I concluded to enjoy the music where we were and he and Sister P— sang through their list.

February 16, 1864.

Mrs. Doolittle's school commenced to-day in the chapel, with about fifty scholars, a grand thing for our soldiers, and Miss Low's box of books arrived just in time. Sister Griggs has received a donation of sixty dollars from a young ladies' seminary in Wheeling, W. Va., for rocking chairs and footstools for her ward, and her friend who has charge of it suggests acknowledgments by letters from the soldiers to them. As Sister G— has promised us a chair, of which we are much in need, she expects some letters to be forthcoming from our ward, so read the accompanying letters to those likely to be interested, hoping some one would write. Sent a note to Dr. Storrs at Willard's. By invitation of dear Mrs. Ripley went to Willard's Hall to see the fine tableaux arranged by Mrs. Bartlett, of Boston, for the benefit of the "Sanitary." They were the most beautiful I ever saw. Excessively cold winter again.

February 17, 1864. Dispatched note to Dr. Storrs by orderly that we would be more than happy to hear a lecture from him in our little chapel. Finished my piece for him entitled "The Shadow at Christmas." As No. 19 had spent the morning in a vain effort to write a note of thanks for the rocking chair, I took his paper and much to his relief wrote one in rhyme, which seemed to delight him much, and he copied it with enthusiasm. Here is the letter:

NO. 19's LETTER OF THANKS

Dear Sally Tingle,
Your name will jingle,
So I will write in rhymes;
What I wish to say
Without delay,

> That we thank you a thousand times.
> For your kindness rare,
> With the rocking chair,
> That has fallen to our lot,
> In which we will sit,
> And think a good bit
> Of you, and no knowing what not.
> The soldiers, you know,
> Though stern to their foe,
> The ladies ever hold dear.
> Excuse the plain speech
> Of your friend William Leech,
>
> A Wisconsin Third Volunteer.

To-day was the most severely cold day we have had this winter, and was obliged to wear my thick cloak and hood all day. Dr. Storrs's lecture on "Trifles" was, as I expected, finished and beautiful, closing with an exquisite tribute to woman. Expected Messrs. Parsons and Martini to delight us with their music, but the excessive cold prevented their coming, and the assembled audience was obliged to content themselves with such entertainment as we could furnish. Because of the intense cold stayed up very late before retiring. At midnight borrowed some flannel costumes from Miss Low's box, which had just arrived. Sisters Griggs and Platt and myself took a hot whisky punch, when we ventured to take off a few outer garments and retire for the night.

February 18, 1864.

The ward was unusually comfortable. C took his papers to Colonel Wisewall, who told him to come again in two days to be examined. Dahle (my last summer's No. 6) came in, being on his way to the front with deserters. I am quite ill with influenza and half starved. Played backgammon in the evening with No. 6, being too stupid or weak for anything else, while C— studied history and the Constitution. Took tea with Miss Low at the "Chateau."

February 19, 1864.

Being starved and chilled, consequently am cross. Sent No. 6 for a stew of hot oysters at ten o'clock and left for the "Home," where he soon followed me with them, and I found they were the medicine I needed. Took a siesta and did not return to the ward until supper time. After I had given out Special Diet I returned to take tea with Miss Low and Mrs. Ripley. Spent part of the evening with Sister Platt, where I found the wife of her "No. 6" and her baby. Curtiss played accompaniments on his guitar and we sang, always assured of a delighted audience of soldier patients in bed, weary of their slowly healing wounds.

February 20, 1864.

Weather moderating. Inspection at four by officer of day, Dr. Horsey. In Ward C Mr. McCloud gave a reading. He proved to be the gentleman I met at Speaker Colfax's reception. He entertained us very pleasantly for an hour.

February 21, 1864.

A quiet morning; no inspection to anticipate, and after making out diet list went to church (Trinity). Dined with Mrs. Wand children in the surgeon's dining room (having invited myself) as "Johnny" (who waits upon our table) had nothing for me. Attended the services in Wards C and E, and finding them not so interesting as usual and very weary, went to our "Home." and slept until after supper time. There were services in our chapel and a sermon.

February 22, 1864.

To-day is Washington's birthday. Misses Low and Lowell left for the front, with the anticipation of attending the "ball" also—quite the envy of the rest. When I entered the ward found Patterson had been proclaimed Ward Master, and worried all day about selecting a No. 6 for orderly. Sister Griggs and I proposed a "candy pull" to celebrate the day, and went to the officer of day (who proved to be Dr. Stuart) for a written order for the "Special Diet Kitchen," which he kindly furnished without any "ifs." We concluded we would prefer having Dr. Bliss's indorsement; therefore dispatched Sister Southwick to the fair, where she found him and obtained it with the timely advice to "pull away." Enjoyed the evening vastly, which proved to be quite a success. Dr. Banister, Drs, Stuart and Horsey, and Lieutenant Colonel Millett were the invited guests. Dr. B went for the two violinists (soldiers), and we had a dance while the candy was boiling, and finished with the "Lancers"; while it must be confessed I enjoyed two fine " Schottisches " with Dr. Horsey, something I never expected to do in this place, but we are really becoming quite conventional and worldly. Dr. S— proved himself an adept in "pulling," and Dr. H— in eating.

We assisted in the braiding, and only reached our "Chateau" at 12 P.M., yet were not demoralized in the least.

February 23, 1864. Sent Dr. Bliss some candy, with the compliments of the "Pullers." Lovely day to-day. Renewed rent of our piano. With "Fees," my new orderly, accomplished the morning duties, and then decided to send for the trained "No. 6 " offered me, hoping the turbulent spirits in the ward would be quiet. Took a charming ambulance drive to the Freedman's Village and Arlington House again, for Dr. Horsey's benefit, who accompanied us and made himself very agreeable and quite entertaining. Went first to the Provost Marshal's for our pass, when Colonel Montgomery kindly gave us a special one for a month. As we arrived home after tea time Dr. H— took tea with us; spent a part of the evening with dear Mrs. Ripley.

Found C— on the antagonistic side, and that his examination was deferred yet another day.

February 24, 1864.

Went to my ward before breakfast and gave out "Special Diet," and to the officer of day for an order for a cup of beef tea. Neither he nor his relief officer, Dr. Stearn nor Dr. Robbins was there, and meeting Dr. Banister, he volunteered to take it to Dr. Stuart, who had not left his room, and considering the length of tape I had used and the color, the ruling spirit of the "Special Diet Kitchen" was obliged to be satisfied with it. I took upon myself a little dignity, though felt like throwing down arms and running away, leaving the place to my antagonists. Mended our "bags," which we have buttoned over the thin bar across the top of each patient's bed. Shortly after diet was attended to, No. 21 suddenly had an epileptic fit, and the young Catholic priest and a woman from one of the relief societies being on hand, both were extremely interested and I suppose thought me extremely cool, as I am becoming quite automaton-like in my manner. Received another note from dear Dr. Storrs and by the afternoon's mail a package of his Drum *Beat* for those who contributed. Misses Low and Lowell returned from the front and gave us interesting descriptions of the Army, of General Meade's review of the cavalry, artillery, etc., and of the grand ball. Mild, but windy and dusty. C— reported himself half examined and continues his studies.

February 25, 1864.

Went to Christian Commission to see if they could furnish a chaplain for us next Sunday morning. Had a call and long chat with Dr. Bowen, who surprised us to-day with his sudden appearance. Miss Thomas and friend, with a contralto voice, gave quite a concert in the ward before supper, and, as usual, drew a crowd.

Found Chad returned a little discouraged, not having yet been examined, so took my tea to the "Home," to be eaten after my return, and made a call on Colonel W, who gave me a written request to Dr. Bliss to allow him to come early and promised to take him before the examining board.

February 26, 1864.

Wrote letter to Sister Gulie; attended the Christian Commission Fair in the evening with six of the "Sisters." We were astonished by the arrival of a new lady nurse, very sweet and interesting, Miss Merrill, of Portland, who has been at Fort Schuyler nine months. C— was examined, but has not received the decision. The *Drum Beat* comes regularly.

February 27, 1864.

My new No. 6 is quite ill, and had but a few moments' rest at the "Home," before I was obliged to return to the ward to give out the evening medicine. Practiced a while after supper. On my way to

Sister S—'s ward met Dr. Banister, who admits he's lonely since Sister Griggs went to Baltimore on Thursday and accompanied me; found her Irish violinist had returned and was making the ward lively with his music. Lieutenant Colonel Millett came in also, and we spent the rest of the evening. Sad letter from Jobes, our first ward master, who has lost one of his children.

February 28, 1864.

Inspection for the last time on this day, as Dr. B— was engaged at the fair yesterday. Our ward received an anticipated compliment, it being the first inspection since Patterson has been ward master. No. 6 is still ill and obliged to do all my work without assistance. Went with Miss Hill to evening service in the Chapel, which proved to be a Methodist prayer meeting. Received Yonkers paper with description of the wonderful "Sanitary Fair" in Brooklyn, N. Y.

February 29, 1864.

On going to my ward found my new No. 6 with bag in hand ready to take his departure, as Dr. Stuart had been in and finding him ill had transferred him to Ward H again, and made a short rounds, probably not wishing to see me. The ward generally was in a state of quiescence. Patterson came with the keys and so troubled that I forgave him even the slight satisfaction that I thought he felt yesterday. I expressed myself in a few words and finished the diet requisition, and my morning duties in short order, too, and left; spent the rest at our "Home." Wrote a valentine for Sister S— to send to the Lieutenant Colonel and a letter for Gulie to put in the post office at the great fair. Dr. Bliss came in with his train of clerks and the muster rolls, just as I finished giving out the medicine. Patterson acting No. 6 I endeavored to sleep away the afternoon. Found Dr. Smith in the ward when I went to give out the evening medicine; felt miserable and consulted Dr. Banister, who kindly prescribed for me.

Sister S— came with Mrs. Read, whom, *entre nous* [Fr. *between us*], dear Journal, I think a bore. Left the keys with Patterson and went "Home," where I found Miss Merrill, who looked so attractive and related her experiences so pleasantly that we prolonged our talk for a half hour.

March 1, 1864.

Snow and sleet; anything but spring-like. Sent for Johnny H— to bring my breakfast, and went to my ward quite late. Two gentlemen from Brooklyn, Alderman Booth and Rev. Woodworth (Methodist clergyman), made me a pleasant call of a few moments; as I was giving out the medicines I could not talk with them as long as I would have done, so they left with a "God bless you," for which kind words I felt grateful, having need of them to revive my energies today. Among the visitors of all kinds who come here daily is a woman, who modestly requested our *carte-devisites,* and a "slight sketch" of the ladies here, to form and illustrate a book, which she wishes to arrange, and entitle "Heroic Women of this War," which was, of course, declined. Our wards were disturbed by the examining board, and as usual we shall probably lose some of our most important men. I spent a quiet evening reading and talking to some of my suffering patients. Dr. Bowen came at "Taps" to the "Home," and made us a short visit.

March 2, 1864.

Orders came for five of our Ward E soldiers to be returned to duty, among them Kysor, our "dresser" and our "rustic frame maker," who is too ill to go. The doctor has made a special application for the former, in which I have not the slightest faith, as we have never been able to keep one yet. Sister Griggs returned from Baltimore and brought us a beautiful cake, made for us and with inscription of icing, "For the Ladies of Armory Square Hospital."

March 3, 1864.

No "No. G " yet, and Kysor was obliged to go with the rest, much to Patterson's regret, who seems to regard him as a brother, being from the same town, and after parting with him at the gate, before the crowd assembled there with a soldier's heart and dry eye, in his own room could not restrain even the tears. Patter-son's stiff shoulder, from the effects of a severe wound, keeps him on hospital duty, fortunately for us. Our frame-maker was reexamined and retained. There was a fine concert in the evening in Ward A by two violinists, two flutists, and a pianist; they also sang comic songs. Kysor and Cross-man (our night watch) returned from the Soldier's Retreat, where they were taken, to spend their last evening here with their friends, and had a merry time in the ward master's room. Sister S— and I wrote a letter of remembrance to Lieutenant Colonel Fox to send by Kysor, who belongs to his regiment.

March 4, 1864.

Found seven of our patients had left in the early train, having received their furloughs, and Natze his discharge papers, so the ward seemed very quiet and empty. One new patient was brought by his mother, who has been trying to take care of him outside, and promises to be quite a nuisance. This was an exciting evening as C received his commission as lieutenant. I examined his papers with him. Colonel W and Mrs. Lampson came in, the former "to see if my sergeant had received his papers." C— came forward and acknowledged the receipt of them, and Colonel W— had neither the sense nor good feeling to congratulate him, which disappointed me. Perhaps army rules would not allow it. This evening being the anniversary of Sister Platt's arrival here, we celebrated it after "Taps." Sister Griggs's cake was cut, and with a hot punch, as Sister P— is suffering from a severe cold, we tried to be merry.

March 5, 1864.

This was a rainy day. Busy all day in my ward as I have no "No. 6." I have decided not to accompany C— to Colonel W's office as he requested. Received a visit from Dr. Jenkins. Inspection at four by little Dr. Munger, officer of day, as Dr. B— was engaged, which Patterson and I regretted as we looked so fine. Went to the chapel in the evening with the choir to practice their church music.

March 6, 1864.

Attended church at the Epiphany, but did not hear Rev. Dr. Hall. Dined at the officers' table, where I found a whole turkey awaiting the commissary's family. Went to my ward, distributed papers and kind words, then home where I enjoyed a bath and siesta. I went to the chapel in the evening expecting to hear a sermon and have a regular service, but it proved to be a Methodist prayer meeting, which I do not enjoy.

March 7, 1864.

To-day was a miserable one. Feeling quite ill, I went on the avenue to get something to eat, it being one of my starvation days. Sister G had received a box and on my return treated me to some mince pie, etc. Took tea at our "Chateau" with four of the sisters, but did not return to the ward, having a headache, and retired early.

March 8, 1864.

Another rainy day. Discussed the important question of allowing "Brady" (the "Daguerreotyper") [famed photographer, Mathew Brady] to take our pictures in a group, but much to my disappointment it was decided not have them taken, fearing they would be made too public, and instead suggested taking a patient from each ward to form a group. C— received his discharge papers.

March 9, 1864.

A beautiful spring day. Our ward being exceedingly quiet and empty I was invited to the ward master's room to see C—'s sword, who left to-day for his boarding house. Went to the Capitol with Sisters Platt and Griggs and Mrs. Ingersoll; met Mr. Lovejoy, who said Garrett Davis was screaming away in the Senate; so Sister G and I went to the House, where they were "throwing cannon balls at one another," but finding it not very interesting, wandered about the Capitol enjoying the fresco paintings, etc., and walked home leisurely, enjoying the fresh air. Found Mrs. Green at the "Home," asking for some lint for the wife of a refugee, who has sacrificed his property and is now very destitute and suffering. Remembered that some of cousin Fannie's contribution was still left I gave it to her. After tea went to the contraband quarters with Miss Merrill to teach them, and was quite interested; the poor creatures are so anxious to learn that it makes my heart ache to see them. I found Sister Southwick there also, with a colored baby on her lap (rather too much for me), and a child on each side reading. Remained after the others left to hear a boy of sixteen read, who came as we were going and looked disappointed thereat. Walked into a mudpool in returning to my ward, and was obliged to go to the "Chateau" for a change. There was a fine concert in Ward A, Miss Thomas and two gentlemen singing with her. An elderly gentleman and his son and daughter also gave us some beautiful music, playing on piano, violin, and flute. A large audience present as usual. Retired early.

March 10, 1864.

Rain again fell to-day. A medical cadet (from Philadelphia) reported to our ward for dresser. C— came in and spent the morning with us, and read to me his congratulatory letter from his father. Two new patients from the invalid corps.

March 11, 1864.

Still another day of rain. As there was so little to detain me in the ward, I spent part of the morning and afternoon at the "Home." C— came about 3 P.M in full uniform and looked extremely well. He had reported, and was immediately ordered to "Meridian Hall." Borrowed some music of Miss Wilson and practiced all the evening.

March 12, 1864.

Beautifully bright day after the rain. Indisposed in the afternoon and did not go to inspection, which was not regretted when I learned Dr. Bliss was not there. By Sister Hill's invitation, had tea at the "Home" with her and Miss Marsh for company. The latter has been to her ward for a few moments to-day for the first time in a week. Spent the evening quietly, excepting a few moments at the chaplain's to thank Mrs. J for the dock root, when I found the lieutenant colonel very amiable, so that he gave me his *carte-de-visite*. I was disturbed the second time after retiring by a call for beef tea for Governor "Hicks," who is dangerously ill at the National Hotel with erysipelas in one of his legs, which has been or is to be amputated. The beef-tea joke was fully enjoyed, as that subject has become farcical.

March 13, 1864.

Attended Dr. Hall's church (Epiphany) with Miss Merrill. He gave us an interesting and beautiful sermon, which I enjoyed in spite of my weariness. The dark clouds passed away and the day was fine. Was delighted to find Captain John Lorimer Worden's card on my return and hope to see him before he leaves town. Received the extra *Drum Beat,* for which we all looked with interest, and was disappointed to find that my "Christmas Shadow" was the only contribution from Armory Square printed in it. Dr. Storrs requested so many, probably had a surplus. Attended evening service at the chapel, which the chaplain said would be conducted by an Episcopal clergyman; but, as usual, it was a special prayer meeting.

March 14, 1864.

Kysor made us a call on his way to Tennessee (having been to "Camp Distribution") fully equipped for marching. He took one of his "hard tacks" from his haversack and gave it to me to remember him. There was a reading in the evening at the chapel by some one (we could not learn his name) who recited part of the "Lady of Lyons." I did not attend. Answered Sarah's letter in Sister Griggs's room. My rustic picture frame (made from a cigar box) is completed, and is the prettiest one I have seen yet. Have also received a number of little presents from my soldiers—among them a heart and cross, carved from ivory, from a new patient.

March 15, 1864.

Dahle called to see us. Went to see "Greene" in Ward S, and the birds; he has put them together and they have built a nest. I also went to see Dr. Robbins about inviting Colonel Straight, late from Libby Prison, to lecture for us. Sister Griggs's father arrived from Brookline, Mass. Lieutenant C came to the hospital about eleven, and after dinner to the "Chateau" to pay his respects to the ladies. Received a letter from Cousin Carrie Vanderburgh saying I was to receive a box from dear old Quaker Hill, which gave me great pleasure, for the remembrance as well as the anticipation of the good things which I know will be in it. Found a large slice of cake on my table from the one sent by the fair to the soldiers who had assisted them. Patterson brought me a treat of raw oysters for my supper. Sergeant Reed returned from furlough. Sister S— and Lieutenant Colonel Millett paid me an evening visit, as did also Dr. Robbins. Wrote a letter to Gulie. My new patient is in a dangerous condition from an operation performed this morning.

March 16, 1864.

My boy with the measles is not so well to-day as it is settling on his lungs. The soldiers were paid. Found cousin Fannie's "oatmeal" just the thing for No. 2, who is in a critical state, although the operation has been very successful thus far. I was surprised by a visit from Uncle Jas I was giving out the evening medicines. Sister Griggs's father took tea with us. No. 49 left for his far-off home in Michigan, scarcely able to walk, but all agreed in believing it might be the best thing for him as he has been ill so long, and the change of air might renovate and strengthen him. Crossman, who has devoted himself to him (being also from Michigan), arranged his things. I prepared him a bottle of the medicine which, with the careful nursing and under God's providence, has saved his life. Was glad to find that he is to have the company of Miss Platt's Indiana boy, who is going in the same train, and who, although on crutches, will be a great comfort to him. My box arrived and I spent the evening disposing of its contents. Sister Griggs thought I had a "hippopotamus" to stow away, and I thought so too before I finished, late and weary.

March 17, 1864.

"Hospital cleaning" commenced in Ward E. Decided I could not go to Fort Sumner to-day and Sister G deferred until to-morrow. Had my small things taken to the "Chateau." Craig finished me a beautiful frame, and I gave him the light vest and pantaloons, with which he was very much pleased. Charlie M— presented me with the things he drew at the fair. My "Special Diet" patients were transferred to Ward F, where I went to assist Sister Hill to make out their diet for to-morrow; the others were distributed, excepting twelve, who remained in the ward. Lieutenant C— came in unexpectedly and I invited him to lunch with me at the "Chateau." Mrs. Ripley concluded to leave in the five o'clock train, so she was obliged to take her tea before us, at our "Home," and our general tea party in her honor was enjoyed after she left. Miss Francis (who is a niece of L. Maria Child [Lydia Maria Child, famous abolitionist and women's rights advocate]) and I accompanied her to the cars, and enjoyed the fresh air in a comfortable barouche. I regretted so much to have her leave, as I have become deeply attached to her. As she requested, gave her the little "Directory," with two additional verses dedicated to her. After the tea things were disposed of, I spent two hours alone at the "Home," deliciously silent; then paid my desolate-looking ward a visit and found the remaining occupants (to whom I had sent a fine addition to their supper), with hats on, collected about the only stove in the room with fire up. Visited my patients in Ward F. Among them the poor little boy ill with the measles, whom I could scarcely make comprehend that neither Sister Hill nor I wished any return for taking care of him. He said so touchingly, "I have a mother." Wrote in journal and retired late.

March 18, 1864.

Went to the commissary's office before breakfast to request the ambulance, which in spite of my diplomatic efforts was " positively engaged " and could not be obtained; but in an hour word came that I could have it, not being aware that I was Sister Griggs's "diplomat," who with her father, Dr. Banister, Sister Southwick, Lieutenant Colonel Millett, and myself formed a very pleasant party. We took our luncheon with us and rode to the Chain Bridge and to Fort Sumner; then called on Miss Griggs's cousin, Lieutenant Colonel Talbot, of the First Maine Artillery, formerly Eighteenth Massachusetts Volunteers. Mrs. Talbot had gone to town. We remained in his small house, from which we had a fine view of their parade ground and saw him and Colonel Chaplain review the regiment. We drove about the fort. It was exceedingly windy and dusty, and it required a great deal of management to keep comfortable. We ate our lunch and altogether we were the merriest party yet, and on our return accepted the lieutenant colonel's invitation to stop in Georgetown for an oyster supper. In the evening there was a concert in Ward A for Mr. Griggs's benefit. Miss Thomas and friends and the lieutenant colonel came, all still in excellent spirits; Lieutenant C— was also present. Retired quite fatigued.

March 19, 1864.

Craig oiled my frame and put the glass in. I packed it in the box to send home by Mr. G, and wrote a long letter. Sister S— being ill, I dined at the "Home," and made tea for her, while vainly trying to ignore my own aching head. However, I persisted in arranging my dress for Mrs. John B. Allen's reception. Lieutenant Colonel M— ordered a carriage and took Sisters S—, Griggs, Platt, and myself. Dr. Robbins accompanied the rest of the ladies, as Mrs. Allen's kind invitation was accepted unanimously.

March 20, 1864.

Quite miserable, and spent the day at the "Home." Made a desperate effort and went to the chapel in loose dress and cloak as we had our first Episcopal service. Mr. Lovejoy called, and Captain John Lorimer Norden (the husband of our old friend and neighbor) spent an hour with me. He is here attending Admiral Wilkes's court-martial and will remain some time. Went to visit Sister Hill and my patients in Ward F in the evening. Dr. S— and Sister H— both prescribed for my nervous headache. Talked a while with my poor boy with the measles, who is very ill; we have promised to telegraph for his mother in the morning. Went to Ward G and joined in the singing; Sister Platt played the melodeon. Colonel Harris and Lieutenant Morton, Sixth Maine, were among the singers, this being their first visit out of Ward K.

March 21, 1864.

Severe cold weather again. Was surprised to hear that our measles boy died at 4 A.M. Went to the ward and wrote a letter to his mother. Too busy about many things to realize that I am "off duty," as our ward is being renovated. Spent the evening in Wards F and C. Mrs. Hall brought in a gentleman formerly from Yonkers and who was organist in Rev. Mr. Brewer's church the first winter we attended.

March 22, 1864.

Commenced letter for Mrs. Daggett. Equinoctial snow storm. Wrote note to Lieutenant Colonel M—who came to see me after dinner and escorted Sister Griggs and myself to the President's reception. Lieutenant C— also came and made quite a visit. Sergeant Harris came to say "good-by." Went to reception notwithstanding the snowstorm. Dr. Robbins escorted the other "Sisters" excepting Misses Platt, Southwick, and Francis. Enjoyed the evening very much. Misses Merrill, Griggs, and I had the presumption to go to the President [Lincoln visited the hospital frequently], meeting him alone in an outer room, for a second "shake" of his cordial hand and make a short speech, which he received very kindly, calling Miss M— "dear child," and thanking me for my compliment; it was thus we "carried off the palm." Our gallant escort hailed a carriage and we arrived home in style; but we had to plunge through a snow bank to get into the house, where Sister Platt was waiting for us with a pot of whisky punch and cup of tea. Mrs. F—, wife of an editor of one of the Boston papers (a very pretty woman), tried to flirt with the colonel, but he had the good taste to prefer the hospital nurses. The ladies from Dr. Bliss's hospital at Baltimore were there, as were also Miss G-'s friend, Miss Capers, and Miss Kendall, the former looking very handsome in evening dress.

March 23, 1864.

Was obliged to bid adieu to our gallant colonel, who had only of late revealed himself in his true colors as a decided ladies' man, instead of a hardened old bachelor. Superintended Uncle Ben's cleaning of our parlor, etc., and went to Ward C in the evening, as Sister P expected Miss Thomas and friends. Lieutenant C and Sister Griggs also came, and at "Taps" we left for the house, taking Lieutenant C with us, where I treated them to a glass of Catawba and cake.

March 24, 1864.

Wrote all the morning. Sister P— was surprised by a present of a beautiful album from her patients. Fine weather to-day. Went with Sister Griggs to the Senate, as we heard that Senator Charles Sumner was to speak, but was disappointed. Went in the Supreme Court chamber, where some of the old judges, or fudges, were asleep, and the rest looked as though they would be soon; fearing it might be contagious, we passed on to the House of Representatives, where we met Mr. McCloud, who said the Hon. E. Brooks, editor of the New York *Express,* was speaking—he was considered the most eloquent in the House, to which remark our Boston friend added, in her decided tone, "a rank copperhead," one of those men who "use the livery of Heaven in which to serve the devil," which dampened our ardor a little. We found him tall, spare, with one eyeglass, an English-looking man, gesticulating as if in a rage about paper currency. I was not prepossessed in his favor. Called at the Massachusetts relief rooms on our way home. Spent the evening with Miss Merrill in her ward, writing and talking over our hospital experiences. Found Miss Capen with Sister Griggs in the parlor, the former remaining overnight. She seems as amiable and capable as her bright face indicates. She invited me to visit Baltimore with Sister G, which I shall hope to do before I leave Washington. My last day "off duty."

March 25, 1864.

Received a good, long letter from Sister Gulie. After a week's absence, again took possession of my ward, which is beautifully clean and white. Our old patients came in immediately after breakfast, bringing their chairs, and looking as pleased as if they had received a furlough. I was glad to take my seat again at the green-covered table, after Johnny, my drummer boy, had assisted me in taking back my ornaments, pictures, etc., from the "Home." Fish day to-day, so dispensed some of my nice Quaker Hill tongue to my patients. Remained all the afternoon in the ward. Lieutenant C— came for a half hour and read me a long letter from his father. After tea played some pretty music Sergeant Reed brought from home (Dr. Banister invited me to attend church, it being Good Friday, but the severe rain prevented). The sick and wounded began to arrive. We received a cavalry boy, shot on picket duty; his limb was amputated a week since, and one poor fellow breathed his last just at the door, so that all we could do for him was to prepare his body for the grave. One dear little fellow of fourteen, who has been some major's orderly, was brought in Ward K, very ill. They say the army is to move immediately, and report says Lee and his army have disappeared.

March 26, 1864.

Found thirteen new patients in our ward and plenty to do, so did not leave it until dinner. Dr. Bliss complimented us at inspection. Enjoyed an hour by myself in our little parlor, lighted only by the two street lamps in front. Plaited a clean cap for my bonnet to wear to-morrow to church, it being Easter Sunday. Patterson (my ward master) presented me with his *carte de visite*.

March 27, 1864.

Dr. Banister asked if he might accompany me to Dr. Hall's church (Epiphany), to which I, of course, assented. It was an elegant day, with a cloudless sky. The church was crowded, but after waiting a half hour I found a seat. The sermon was an interesting one, and I enjoyed the music and sight of the flowers about the altar ever so much, and also the walk, although it was rather a long one. After dinner I was obliged to rest and sleep. Lieutenant C— came in the evening, and we went to the "Chateau," where we found Sisters Griggs and Southwick, and Dr. Banister (who had found the little mission church closed) sitting in the little parlor by the light of the street lamps, to which we did not object. C— remained a while after "Taps," as he was not to meet his friend until ten, to walk back to camp, three miles away.

March 28, 1864.

Endeavored to entertain my ward in the evening, as poor Leech is getting dispirited, fearing he may be obliged to have his foot taken off, or have a useless one for the rest of his life; it is hard even to anticipate such a thing after ten months' confinement.

March 29, 1864.

Wrote a letter for my new amputation patient, whose mother lives in Thirteenth Street, New York. Lieutenant C came in, but thinks he will not ask for leave of absence just now to visit his home. Was delighted to have Johnny, my drummer boy, put down for furlough;

he went to Dr. Bliss and asked for it himself. Professor McLeod came and gave a reading or recitation in Ward F, which was too dry for the soldiers to enjoy; recitation is not his forte, though he evidently thinks he has talent in that line. It rained again furiously.

Johnny H—, my No. 6, went to the "Home" for my rubbers and umbrella, which I find is necessary, as it leaks so here, especially about our "pipe," that we have no way of drying our feet, and the half of our room over Sister S— 's bed was so wet she was obliged to take refuge in Miss Merrill's room.

March 30, 1864.

Wrote notice of the death of my "measles boy" for the *Gazette*, and in my ward book the names, etc., of my patients, which I have neglected of late. Visited my pet patients in the evening, and devoted myself to the ward generally. After "Taps" sat by the stovepipe ruminating, consequently retired late.

March 31, 1864.

A long, monotonous day, devoted to idle thinking. At night such a miserable decoction of tea on our table that I invited Sister Hill to join me at the "Home," after which took a walk with her and Sister Marsh to the telegraph office. Called at the Newsboys' Home on our return, and was very much pleased to see such nice quarters for them. Went in Ward D to hear Miss Merrill try her new piano. Commenced writing a letter for Quaker Hill.

April 1, 1864.

A real April Fool's day—busy, busy about nothing. It commenced raining again after dinner. Wrote in the evening until midnight, which finished my Quaker Hill document. Miss Capen came from Baltimore to attend reception at Speaker Colfax's, but too rainy.

April 2, 1864.

A most miserable day, raining and snowing together. Was obliged to place five dishes in our room to catch the dripping water. This was a busy day for me. Assisted the ward master in putting up our curtains, and at inspection Dr. Bliss pronounced our ward "perfect," with many compliments. Crossman's wife came from Michigan without giving him warning, and there was quite an affecting scene. Spent the evening in Ward C as Sister Anna Platt's assistant.

April 3, 1864.

Spent the whole morning in my ward, in addition to my usual duties, writing letters and entertaining my "amputation boy," and doing various things too numerous to mention here. Felt the effects of midnight vigils, and took a long sleep after dinner. Went to see the baby in Ward C, the wife of a soldier having been unexpectedly confined here, shortly after tea. When I returned to the ward to arrange the night medicines found Lieutenant Chad been there, and Patterson told him I was at church. The lieutenant's regiment has moved to General Martindale's barracks at the "Circle."

April 4, 1864. It is five months to-day since I returned. I swept and put my room in order, having leisure as usual on Monday morning; and as I was just finishing, with handkerchief on my head, Mrs. Senator Lane and Miss H. Fanning Read called. The former offered consolation by saying she regretted so much she did not think of sending me an invitation to accompany them to Mount Vernon. Found poor "Fees" quite ill, and made him some tea and toast, and went to Dr. Bliss to get a special pass for Crossman, who, manlike, sent his wife, a stranger, to remind me, instead of doing it himself. Patterson quite ill with a cold, so played backgammon to make him forget it. Dahl came in, and amused himself looking on, as I used to play with him last summer. It is raining again.

April 5, 1864.

Rain, rain, rain, and persistently pouring. I felt "dumpish" and took breakfast with Sister Hill, who is indisposed at the "Home"; used Sister Griggs's admirable little arrangement to boil an egg. Then went up and took charge of her ward also, making out "special diet," and arranging medicines for both wards. After dinner had a long and interesting conversation with Miss Merrill, and after going to the "House" spent the rest of the afternoon with her and Sister Platt sewing, the steady rain on the roof shutting out even our wards for a short time.

April 6, 1864.

Four new patients arrived, among them a good violinist. The sun shone at last, and our dampened spirits were cheered up; the afternoon was charming. Took a walk with Sister Platt, and was glad that we relinquished the idea of going to the House of Representatives to hear George Thompson deliver his English sentiments on slavery. As we had a musical evening, our two violinists, with bass viol and piano accompaniment, were playing when Miss Thomas and friends arrived, and we enjoyed some excellent music. Mrs. Davis, a wealthy New York lady, very much interested in the hospitals there, in the fair, etc. (having contributed $1,200 to the fair), came with some friends in our ward to-day and asked permission to converse with the men.

April 7, 1864.

After finishing my morning duties in the ward I copied the music of some of our bugle calls. Sister Griggs, who has spent her week of "off duty" with some friends in town, returned this morning. Received a letter from Mrs. Bradley, a friend of long ago, took a short walk for fresh air, and called at Mr. Blanchard's store, who gave me a rubber ruler. On my return went directly to the ward, where I found, as I expected, Miss Thomas with seven young girls from Mrs. Amidon's school singing with her, which as usual delighted a large crowd from the other wards also, after which the bugle called " Assembly," and the soldiers collected in the open air to hear the great American traveler (as he calls himself), Daniel Pratt, speak, whom they said was very amusing, though some think slightly demented. Went to Ward C a while before "Taps" to try their new piano. Little Johnny left to-day on furlough.

April 8, 1864.

Busy all the morning with one of my new patients who has the measles, and attended to the numberless wants of the others. Wrote account of yesterday's concert for the *Gazette,* at the request of Pyne (one of the young printers), and also a notice of Mrs. Ripley's departure. Went with Sister S— to call on the Misses Gillies.

Miss R— had gone to New York, to attend the fair. Mrs.— and Miss G— were very cordial and gave us a gay little bouquet (they are in charge of the Naval Observatory), which must be very pleasant in summer. Took a promenade past the barracks, at the Circle, to inspect the quarters of the Veteran Reserve Corps, where our friend Lieutenant C— is living. Saw Mrs. Lincoln in her establishment. Found a letter from the mother of my "measles" boy, who died.

April 9, 1864.

More rain, rain, rain. Lieutenant C— called for a few moments before dinner. Dr. Van Dyck inspected to-day. Played dominoes with two of my pet boys, after giving a number of them a nice relish at supper of dried beef and a can of Carrie Vander-burgh's cherries. Went to Ward C, where Sister Anna had gathered the hospital choir, ladies, surgeons, etc. As it was still raining hard, Patterson insisted upon my wearing his raincoat home. Found my room wet, with only one dry corner in it.

April 10, 1864.

Our soldiers were allowed to attend church outside, in charge of an orderly sergeant. The Protestants went to the Capitol to hear Edward Everett Hale [American author, historian, abolitionist and Unitarian minister], and, at the solicitation of the devoted young priest who visited our hospital, the Catholics went to their church. Remained in ward until dinner, although feeling ill and miserable. Most of the ladies went to the chapel in the evening to hear the Hon. Amasa J. Brooks, who was not very interesting. Preferred sitting in the lamplight, after attending to the night medicines in the ward. The proposed visit to the President of Miss Merrill and myself, accompanied by our friends, is not to be, as her young friend came to tell her to-day he was under marching orders—in fact, everything available seems to be.

April 11, 1864.

Am still weak and miserable, but went to the ward to see about the extra orders, there is such a fuss about them. Miss Merrill's and Sister Platt's orders were both returned to them yesterday. Our soldiers were allowed to go to the House to-day to hear Speaker Colfax's resolution to expel Long of Ohio for treasonable words discussed. Wrote letters for my "boys."

April 12, 1864.

Beautiful weather. Lieutenant came in looking as fine as possible, to see about the reception to the President, etc., but, being in a "flyaway" humor, he could not stay a moment. The daughter of Mrs. Jacobs, authoress of "Linda" (her own life when a slave), came to see Miss Francis, whose aunt, Lydia Maria Child, edited the book. She has beautiful eyes and very pleasing manners. I believe she is teaching school. Mr. George Wood called in the evening and brought the *Spirit of the Fair,* the New York paper, which does not promise much. Wrote the following verse for the *Gazette,* which is printed by two young soldiers, and supervised by Mrs. Ingersoll of Maine:

>Spring has come with buds and flower;
>Wakened up by April showers;
>Twilight lingers into even,
>Turning worldly thoughts to Heaven.
>Nature brightening seems to say:
>"Spring has come—why not be gay?"
>Ah! Nature smiles tho' War and Death
>Of home and friends have us bereft,
>And spectre-like on distant hills
>Sit with their train of human ills:
>Tho' War must rage and Death must come,
>To desolate the heart and home.
>Yes! Spring has come and kindly spread
>The soft green carpet for our tread;
>Her light o'er hill and vale is seen,
>But all her charms will fail to wean
>Our hearts to gladness, when so nigh
>The hour to sound the battle-cry.
>We bless her as a friend who comes
>When Death has desolated homes,
>With words of comfort sweetly given
>To lift our eyes from earth to Heaven;

> We bless her, tho' she cannot save,
> She strews the daisies o'er the grave.
> But ask us not with hearts of glee
> To join in Nature's revelry,
> With brooks and birds and gayest flowers
> To pass in thoughtlessness the hours;
> The summer breeze we feel so nigh
> Will also bring the battle-cry.

ARMORY SQUARE,

April, 1864.

April 13, 1864.

My "measles" boy is recovering and the ward is very comfortable. Dr. S—, Patterson, and a number of others wrote to Kysor, to which I added a sheet, making quite a long letter; we also added a " round robin " for our late lamented lieutenant colonel. Went to the "Home" after tea, and sat with Sister Griggs, who is not well, in the lamplight, being indisposed myself. Dr. Banister came in, and soon after Lieutenant C—, who came to see if I would go to Ward G and hear the music being given by Miss Thomas and some friends, who sang a very pretty selection, ending with the " Young Recruit," as usual to the delight of her large audience.

April 14, 1864.

This was a very busy morning, with a multitude of little things to attend to. I was anxious about the new order for the surgeons to make out the discharge papers of all our old wounded patients. After finishing in my ward took the " gruel " which I had made for Sister Griggs and myself to the "Home," hurriedly ate it, and went with Miss Ware (our new lady nurse, who takes Miss Francis's place) to the Capitol, where I succeeded at last in getting a standing place in the doorway, and remained half crushed for two hours; then was pushed to the steps, where I sat for two more hours, intensely interested in both Mr. Col-fax's and Mr. Long's speeches; the former in his usual easy amiable, earnest, clear'-and sometimes eloquent manner; the speech of the latter was dignified and fearless, and bespoke one's sympathy and respect for everything but his misguided views and sympathy with the South. Neither speaker indulged in personalities, in striking contrast with Garrett Davis's vituperation. When I went to the ward I was astounded by the news that Patterson, our ward master, was in the Central Guardhouse; his pass, which he did not observe, had not received the stamped signature of Dr. Bliss, and when asked for it by the patrol, he showed it in all confidence, and was invited by them to go to the Central Guardhouse. He met some of our men and told them of his plight, and fortunately the lieutenant in command of the guardhouse was from our hospital, and knew and freed him immediately from his unpleasant position. Dr. S— went to see about it, too, but found that Patterson was out. I spent the evening with Sister Griggs at the "Home."

April 15, 1864.

After the morning's duties, Dr. S, who plays the violin, asked me to try some music, and we practiced and played together, much to the amusement of our patients. Went on the avenue to change the rubber needle, of which I am to have a chain made. Received a present of a beautiful little bracket with the badges of different army corps carved on it, made by one of my patients, and huge cakes of maple sugar. Sister Southwick decided to go to her home in Boston for a short visit, and left with one of her patients, in charge of a hospital car at five o'clock this evening. After bringing Sister Griggs's tea, I returned to the ward and played dominoes with No. 6. Enjoyed my room, being alone to-night.

April 16, 1864.

Another rainy day. Took leave of Miss Francis, who goes to Baltimore this evening on her way home. Ward E is at the zenith of its glory, for at inspection Dr. Bliss said " it looked elegant," the floor was so white; and on his return, after telling the other ward masters to go and look at the floor and beds in E, told me that we took the palm from all the other wards. All this, I must confess, gave me a little pleasure to repeat at the tea table, and I feel that much of the praise is due to Patterson, our faithful and efficient ward master. In the evening, after giving my "boys" some music, went to Ward G and played for Miss Marsh, who has taken the piano from Ward K.

April 17, 1864.

Still showery. My "measles" boy is out of bed, so I have very little to be anxious about in my ward. Sergeant Reed and Kenser have received their discharge, and nearly all my old patients will soon be obliged to leave. It is about time for me to take a rest also. Concluded I was too weak and the weather too "Aprilish" to attend church, so refreshed myself by taking a "nap." In the afternoon I accompanied Sister Griggs and Dr. Banister to hear Dr. Baxter, who considers it his mission to tell us of the coming "Tribulation and the Battle of Armigeddon," etc. I was interested but not converted to his peculiar views in reference to Louis Napoleon, etc. He preached in a church for colored people, and although half of the audience to-day were white, I was quite interested in the other half. After leaving church I witnessed a dress parade of some of the Veteran Reserve Corps stationed near by, reminding us that the army enjoyed very few Sabbaths. A fine, moonlight evening.

April 18, 1864.

One of my driving days. Went to see Mrs. Sampson about Brownell's furlough, as he is so anxious to meet his brother in New York. Was constantly interrupted while attending to morning duties. Received four of Ward D's patients, as they have broken up camp to-day. Went to the "Chateau," but found the workmen on our roof hammering with such violence, tearing off the old tarred paper and bringing down clouds of dirt and whitewash, etc., that I beat a retreat, and having nowhere else to go, took some marrow into the chaplain's and asked Mrs. J to allow me to make my salve there. Read "Linda" while waiting for it to cool. Received my hat box from home and enjoyed its contents. Branch (my old "amputation boy " with a wooden leg, who has of late acted like the "old boy," having a few nights since climbed over and back the high fence topped with pickets about us) came down on his crutches to tell me that Miss Thomas wished to see me. I found her, and Miss Yateman also, who invited me, with Sister Griggs and Dr. Banister, to spend to-morrow evening at their house. Enjoyed some of the biscuits from home for my tea. Lieutenant C— came in for a few moments, being engaged to accompany some of his brother officers to a ball at Cliff-burn Barracks. Found our house without a fire, consequently it was so comfortless, I went in pursuit of the general ward master and general night watch, and by ten o'clock obtained a little heat in the house. Miss Low's alcohol lamp and a cup of hot tea were our sole dependence for warmth. Mrs. Jackson came in to ask the favor of Sister S—'s vacant bed for her sister, which I was happy to accord her for past favors.

April 19, 1864.

Sent orderly with note to see about Sister Southwick's box, which I was glad to find was safe and already expressed to her. Sister G— came in to say that the reception by the President would be held that evening, so hurried through my morning duties. After dinner I prepared some things for the evening, and wore the pink dress, etc., my sisters kindly sent me.

Sister G's cousin came for us, Dr. Robbins for some of the ladies, and Miss Merrill's young soldier for her. We went at nine, and found more of a crowd than on New Year Day, and were more than an hour getting from the pavement to the President's hand. At the close of the evening Mrs. Lincoln made the tour of the East Room with General [future President James] Garfield and the President, and a young lady whose name we did not ascertain. The flowers in the unique vases were superb. Reached home ever so weary. Sister G— offered me a hot punch, which I was glad to take, and then hurried to bed.

April 20, 1864.

Spent the day in bed, not having sufficient strength or energy to get up. Read the whole of "Linda" from the beginning to the end, and found plenty of time to think besides. Later made "an effort," remembering Mrs. Chick's advice to Mrs. Dombey, put on a gown, and took tea with Sister Hill, who was also indisposed in the next room. Sister Griggs soon made one of our party, and Mr. George

Wood, who lent us his "Peter Schlemyl" a few days since, came in and spent the evening. Was surprised to receive Mr. Ramsdell's wedding cards.

April 21, 1864.

Arose bright and early, as the ladies reported more patients have arrived, and were still arriving when they left their wards, in all, about one hundred. I found we had seven, four very ill, and have of course been busy all day, having nineteen on special diet, and having given out over a hundred doses of medicine. One poor man, I fear, will never recover. Became disgusted and indignant about the beef tea arrangement, and after a visit to the special kitchen spoke my mind freely at our dinner table. Whereupon Miss L—, who has charge of the special diet kitchen, left suddenly, like a gust of wind, and making only a slight rustle. I suspected she was en route for the surgeon in charge, so I laid down knife and fork and went after her, my determined step following closely the delicate patter along the long corridor, until she, finding the surgeon had company, turned about. I nevertheless passed in, and asked him to explain to me the necessary process to procure a little beef tea, etc. It was quite an amusing episode. I remained in my ward until three o'clock, then accompanied Miss G— to make our call on the Yatemans (neighbors), to acknowledge their kind invitation. Spent the evening endeavoring to add to the comfort of my four suffering patients, who have evidently not been used to much kindness of late, and are very grateful. Received a serenade from our hospital band.

April 22, 1864. Last evening I suddenly decided that I must have a rest and recruit before this terrible warfare is renewed, and before our wards are again filled with wounded soldiers, as they were last May, after the battle of Chancellorsville. Dr. Bliss, our surgeon in charge, has kindly given me leave of absence, so I take a morning train to-morrow for New York. Happy thought!

May 6, 1864.

Left home again at 6 P.M., for Washington and hospital life, having received such a definite opinion from our surgeon in charge that I thought it best to make an appearance in Ward E before inspection to-morrow. My sisters accompanied me to the ferry, where Mr. Ogden met us. The night wore away at last, and at 6 A.M. I reached Washington, took a city car, and soon walked into Ward E, where I surprised them making the beds, but received a very pleasant welcome. I went to the ladies' "Chateau," and giving a loud rap on the door Sister Hill came out and said, "I know Sister Akin has come," at which Sister Griggs came out *en deshabille* with her kind welcome.

During my absence "Spring has passed down the vale, left her robe on the trees and her scent on the gale." The Smithsonian grounds seem in full leaf, and the grass and flowers between our wards, as there was none last summer, appear more beautiful to my eyes than anything else outside. I took breakfast, made hasty improvements in my toilet, and went to perform my morning duties in the ward. After shaking hands with all my old patients, I saw Dr. Bliss in passing the office; he greeted me pleasantly, and as soon as he came in the ward I made an apology for my prolonged absence, which he received graciously.

After dinner was obliged to sweep my room before taking the rest so much needed. It is like midsummer weather outside. After tea gave my men some music, though I was glad I made arrangements to retire early for the night.

May 8, 1864.

Another hot day. Dr. Kennan is my surgeon *pro tem*. After dinner attended funeral services in the chapel of a soldier from Ward K. We have news of a battle in which General Grant is not only victorious, but is pursuing General Lee, and that one thousand wounded will be at the station to-night, whom our committee has orders to feed. We also hear that General Butler has routed Beauregard.

May 9, 1864.

None of our wounded is heard from, and fears are entertained that the guerrillas have intercepted them. Dr. Kennan reported ill, and Dr. Brinte made the rounds. Received a young lady, Miss Cheney from Boston (introduced by the Hon. Mr. Lovejoy), who is anxious to be one of our sisterhood. The ward master received a note from Lieutenant C—, which was sent by one of his men, saying he was in command of a company at Chain Bridge, and it might be some time before he could pay us a visit. Two hundred and fifty slightly wounded arrived who gave thrilling accounts of their falling in the hands of the rebels at Fredericksburg, while on their way here. The most severely wounded are still there, unable to escape. Supper was given to them in the cook-house, and some of them were sent to different wards. When they had passed through their ablutions and were ready for bed an order came that they were to go immediately to Carver Hospital. Fortunately none was sent into our ward, but Sister Hill was obliged to beg that a few might be allowed to remain. Dr. Bliss introduced our new surgeon, Dr. Hurlburt, who made his rounds and seemed unusually pleasant. Dr. Bowen also arrived this evening with two other new surgeons.

There is a report of Colonel Millett's death, but we refuse to believe it. One of the Fifth Maine soldiers says he saw him charging at the head of a column; heart-sickening thought, though we cannot but admire the courage which meets this awful necessity.

May 10, 1864.

There is still no permanent surgeon; Dr. Brinte made the rounds. Received a call from Miss Gillies and an army officer, who brought me a basket of beautiful flowers and two large dishes of blancmange. After tea, arranged myself in my new full uniform, and went with Sister Hill to call upon Mr. and Mrs. Ramsdell, our head clerk and his bride, who are living opposite the Smithsonian.

May 11, 1864.

Received an early call from a Brooklyn lady with a note from Dr. Storrs asking me to aid her to find her son (Sergeant O'Connor) among the wounded of the late battle. Went with her to Ward F, where a few of them were allowed to remain, but failed to find him. Took her to breakfast, and, after leaving directions and executive order with No. 6, accompanied her to Carver Hospital, where we found him. He was slightly wounded in the head, and was a very intelligent man, who gave us a minute account of his journey from the battlefield, fighting with the guerrillas, etc., and showed us the slippers he wore all the way, having given his gaiters to his lieutenant. We also met an interesting soldier in the car, Lewis Bradley, of Newburgh, who said General Sedgwick's remains came up that morning with him.

Returning, on my way to the ward I met Lieutenant Conyers coming in the gate; he remained a half hour. The wounded were coming in all day. One ward received fifty, and a thousand more are expected to-morrow. Dr. Munger was assigned to our ward. Received a letter from Leech (No. 17 so long) and a pretty present of an ornament of spun glass from my musical German, Graffleman, formerly employed in a glass factory in New Jersey and just returned from furlough. Was sorry to hear that young Best, who occupied the bed next to my table for a month, was the first man killed in his company.

May 12, 1864.

There was a severe thundershower after dinner, and the ambulances were passing and stopping all day. All who came to our ward yesterday, excepting four, were but slightly wounded, and, with a few convalescents, were transferred to a tent ward. Received six more severely wounded patients, two lieutenants and two sergeants. There was one amputation after dinner.

Went with Sister Griggs to see Brigadier General Sedgwick's remains, but found only Brigadier Generals Hayes and Stephenson and Colonel Chapman at the embalmer's. General Sedgwick's body was sent North last evening. Sister Southwick is at last really going to the front with Miss H. Fanning Read, who obtained a pass for her from the surgeon general to Fredericksburg, tomorrow. Received a present of a beautiful bouquet from my young Bohemian night watch.

May 13, 1864.

Our attendants, etc., were up all night bringing in and taking care of the wounded, who have been coming in all day.

We received twenty-eight new patients, among them Major Draper, of the Thirty-sixth Massachusetts, and Captain Dwight, One Hundred and Twenty-second New York, and two rebels—one a conscript; the other seems to have enlisted from a serious conviction of duty; he has been in eight battles, but is pleasantly disposed and reconciled to his fate, unlike the others I have seen.

It made me feel sick and weak when I went into the ward to see almost every bed filled with a new patient and with a ghastly wound. Fortunately it was a rainy day, and Sister S— and Miss R— could not leave to-day. Mr. Fuller, a New York agent, who came from Fredericksburg, was in here, and says that the corduroy road from Belle Plain to Fredericksburg is in very bad condition, and many of the wounded are lying in the streets, and the people there (mostly Secessionists) will not furnish them with either food or bandages.

Have thirty patients on special diet, for whom I was obliged to prescribe, as the surgeon has two more tent wards. Mrs. Senator Lane (our early friend) brought newspapers and oranges.

May 14, 1864.

Sister Southwick left for the front. Major Draper's wife arrived. She is a lovely woman, and it is quite affecting to see them together. There was no inspection to-day. Mailed a letter home. Miss McClellan, daughter of the Assistant Postmaster General, who is to take Sister Southwick's ward and place in my room, came today. Went to market after tea to get some oranges for Lieutenant Bly, who suffers so much.

May 15, 1864.

Sunday, but had no outward rest. Miss Stephens, daughter of the novelist, and a friend came in with Dr. Bliss.

The Maine Artillery from Fort Sumner passed. It is a fine regiment. Miss Griggs's cousin, Lieutenant Colonel Talbot, was with them; he waved her an adieu as he passed, and I realize now daily the pathos of the "Soldier's Last Farewell."

May 16, 1864. Dr. Bliss examined Lieutenant Bly's arm and said it must be amputated immediately. An exciting day. A new patient, Lieutenant Grenier of the Fifth Maine, a friend of Lieutenant Colonel Millett, arrived. Another new surgeon added to the staff, Dr. Coolidge, of Boston. He is a very pleasant, gentlemanly man; knows nothing of hospital regulations, but has much enthusiasm and sympathy. I was glad to have him attend to many of the patients who I felt were neglected, though his unsystematic way gives us unnecessary work. Went with Sister Griggs to the Smithsonian a few moments before dark, and read a note she had received from Dr. Banister, her former surgeon, who is now at Belle Plain dressing wounds (as the wounded pass there); he has not had his clothes off since he left here.

I fear Lieutenant Bly's hours are numbered. He cannot take stimulants. Sent to Mrs. Senator Lane to purchase a bottle of champagne for him, which she sent without charge. Another artillery regiment passed for the front.

May 17, 1864.

Felt quite ill, but managed to keep about. Received a note from Sister Southwick, who has reached Fredericksburg, and answered it by the Massachusetts agent, who returned to-day. The lieutenant is very low. Was delighted to find we have an assistant chaplain, Rev. Mr. Crocker, who belongs to one of the New York regiments and knows Lieutenant Bly, having belonged to his brigade, the Ninth New York Cavalry.

Dr. Bliss was flying about all day with his case of instruments; he came into our ward and in five minutes extracted a ball from a wound. The weather is fine once more. After tea went to the armory to see how it had been arranged for the wounded; when I returned found Lieutenant Bly's bed had been carried out, for his spirit had suddenly taken flight. Wrote out some of the bed cards which Dr. Munger left for me, as I unfortunately promised to assist him.

May 18, 1864.

Very warm weather again. Fifteen patients transferred to Philadelphia, making a morning of confusion. Being so late from the battlefield, they had no clothes, and we were obliged to draw on our stock here. Supplied many with shirts and stockings from my own store.

Received an amusing letter from "Fees." Misses Thomas and Martin came to the house to see me and offered their services. A very pleasant lady, Mrs. Clark, comes in and really does some good waiting upon the patients who are suffering. She sent me to-day a nice tin tea kettle. Our men sent away in the morning returned before supper, unable to get transportation. I sent them to the armory to sleep, as their beds were made up clean, ready for those expected to-night. We have already received six new patients; they are very low; two have been amputated and three shot through the lungs. One is a poor rebel boy, only eighteen, from Louisiana; he looks so pitiful and grateful for every little kindness which he does not expect.

Retired, worn with the sight and sound of suffering.

May 19, 1864.

This was the most wearisome and exciting day I have had yet. The wounded came at all hours. Dr. Coolidge went through the entire ward making many changes and new prescriptions, and while wondering how I could obtain all of the diet, with unuttered prayers in my heart to be able to do more for their comfort, seeing the need of so much, a letter was brought to me containing a check for one hundred dollars from Mr. Simpson, of Hudson, and his friend Mr. Lamson, of New York. That was too much for overtaxed nerves, and the tears, which had been kept under control amid all I had witnessed for so many days, would come, after which luxury I took up my sad work with renewed spirit and energy. Ladies came in with lemons and oranges; one with lemonade for the whole ward.

Lieutenant Bly's wife arrived this morning, she evidently not having received the last telegram; as the lieutenant's body had been sent home yesterday, she returned immediately to the train, leaving a request with Mrs. Chaplain Jackson that I would be kind enough to write to her. Am happy to find we have an assistant chaplain who is faithful in his duties; he formerly belonged to a New York regiment, the same brigade as Lieutenant Bly. He recognized him, and it was gratifying to see him in prayer by his bedside before his death.

Lieutenant C came, not having returned to the bridge since Tuesday from the barracks in Georgetown. Misses Stephens and Binn came in and brought Mrs. S's last novel and a great variety of papers. With the interruptions, thought I would never get the diet list made out, which was at last sent in at three o'clock. The butter was not fit to eat at supper, and we had it reported; fortunately I had been to the market this morning and purchased some. I went to the "Home" at four to rest a few moments, and after tea to the Smithsonian grounds with Sister Griggs, feeling an oppressive want of fresh air. Played for my men instead of making out bed cards, as I saw them watching my movements, and when I went to the piano they exclaimed, "That's what we want!"

May 20, 1864.

Two of our patients that came in last died to-day, one in the night and one of the amputated men just before dinner Beautiful weather; the tide of visitors was tremendous; Dr. Bliss said there were fifteen hundred at supper-time; it seemed as if I were holding a reception. Miss Welles, daughter of the Secretary of the Navy [Gideon Welles], whom I have not seen since last summer, with a friend, came and offered their services to write letters. Four men from New York and Brooklyn shook hands with me, and one benevolent-looking man parted the hair on my forehead, and, having ascertained that I had no relations in the army, said, "She is here just to do her duty." One lady was singing at the piano and the rest of the visitors promenaded, while I gave out twenty-eight special diets, and amid such a confusion it was difficult to keep my wits. Fortunately our ward had been cleaned thoroughly, the first time in a fortnight.

Mrs. Governor Morgan, a stout lady, with a profusion of diamonds, called in the morning and brought some lemons, etc. Drs. Stuart and

Banister returned to-day; their wards gave them a cordial welcome, and I confess I shall be thankful to see Dr. Stuart in charge of our ward again.

Had a talk with Captain Dwight, who is very modest and pleasant. It is no trouble to wait upon him.

May 21, 1864.

Dr. Coolidge, of Boston, made the morning rounds, but Dr. S— came in the evening. Dr. Bliss denied all visitors who came out of curiosity, at which order we were much relieved. There was no inspection, although many of the ladies went up expecting it. After supper I could not refuse to give my patients some music, although I was very weary, and was glad when Mr. and Mrs. Ramsdell came in and the latter relieved me.

May 22, 1864.

Our duties seem lightened already with Dr. Stuart in the ward. Dr. Coolidge expressed much interest and regret at leaving the patients. The wounded from the First Maine Artillery, which passed so proudly just a week to-day, were brought in and taken to the armory. The whole regiment were in the engagement on Thursday and badly cut up. One soldier with a fractured limb was brought to us.

Having made a chair comfortable with the long cushion I brought from home for my own use, I was glad to see it enjoyed both by Major Draper and Captain Robinson when they were able to sit up. The weather was very warm. I succeeded in dispatching a letter to my good friend, Mr. Simpson, which relieved my mind.

Visitors were generally denied admission, but many went through the wards. The new chaplain held service. Managed to secure a few moments' leisure, and had a pleasant talk with Lieutenant Grenier (convalescent), who gave me his *carte de visite,* and promised to send a cribbage board, etc. No. 44, in whom the chaplain of his regiment and I have been greatly interested, died suddenly before I left.

May 23, 1864.

Captain Dwight of the One Hundred and Twenty-second New York Regiment left for home. Used my gas stove, purchased yesterday. It is certainly a great invention and convenience. Went to our quarters, but could not sleep.

May 24, 1864.

No. 45 very low, and will scarcely survive the night. He dictated a very affecting letter to Assistant Chaplain Crocker for his wife. He is Andrew Twitchell, private, Thirty-sixth Michigan Cavalry. Mr. Clapp and friends from Yonkers called.

May 25, 1864.

Sent an ivory cross a soldier made and a letter to Sister Gulie. More wounded arrived, among them three captains and one lieutenant. Our No. 45 (while I was supporting his head) suddenly breathed his last.

May 27, 1864.

Fifteen patients were transferred to Philadelphia. Others were brought in to fill their places, with still worse wounds, uncared for and unwashed; they were well-nigh dead from the toils of their journey. Wrote a letter for No. 12, who found his brother's name among the wounded at another hospital. Sent No. 6 (my orderly) to hunt him up, who discovered him only to find that he was just carried out for a second amputation. Miss Welles came to write letters, and I managed to write to the wife of No. 45, who died two days since, and to Lieutenant Bly's widow. Returned to the "Home" at 5 P.M.

May 28, 1864.

Major Draper had so improved that he left to join his wife at the hotel. No. 25 died during the night. No. 44 was bleeding and very weak. I went to market, and on my return found ten more wounded had been brought in. Our dresser is tired out. Was all day in the ward, and the air was foul and dreadful. Captain Dewey was very pleasant. Captain Brooks of the Twelfth New Jersey Regiment is like a spoiled child, but he will soon "find his bearings." He told his attendant to tell "her" to make him some lemonade, which I did and sent it by the attendant, with directions, in sufficiently clear tone, to take it to No. 12, after which he called me by name and we became good friends.

A number of patients went to Mount Pleasant Hospital to relieve the crush at our hospital.

May 29 and 30, 1864.

Kept no record of these two days' doings, having neither the time nor the strength.

May 31, 1864.

The arrival of relatives only to find their dear ones had passed " beyond the smiling and the weeping," beyond all pain and weariness, is one of the most unnerving of trials we are called upon to meet. Summer is here, and the stoves were all removed this morning.

I obtained a special pass for Lieutenant Grenier. Borrowed Sister Hill's rolling chair for Captain Robinson, who is convalescing slowly, and went with him to our "Chateau" (as our French friend, Dr. Alcan, calls our domicile), where I treated the captain to claret and crackers. Mrs. Draper called, and I accompanied her to the office, where we found the major, who was quite Chesterfieldian in his manner of bidding adieu. Mrs. Draper gave me his photograph for my album.

Copy of a letter written in hot haste about May 30, 1864, during the Battle of the Wilderness. It was written by Sister Helen Griggs of Ward A to Sister Anna Platt of Ward C, who had left to recruit:

The Battle of the Wilderness was part of General Grant's Overland Campaign, fought May 5–7, 1864, with terrible casualties on both sides.

OUR ROOM, TEN O'CLOCK.

I am tired to death, and an awful "gabbling" going on in the next room, as six new nurses have been engaged temporarily for the extra tent wards; some with dreadful voices. That is the date of my letter.

MY DEAR MRS. METTERNICH:

(As you do not appreciate the Talleyrand title, perhaps you will this.) I have left the man with one elephant in the dim, far distance, as I now have a dozen on my hands, and six dozen on my brain; not elephants, but leviathans and megatheriums—all those big, huge antediluvians that scare you to look at them.

I cannot write a connected letter; I lost my senses two weeks ago and haven't known my own name for a week. I cannot begin to tell you of what we are going through. Miss Hill and Miss Akin say the number of wounded after Chancellorsville was nothing; was mere play to what this is. Oh! they are piled in on us till one's heart sinks, and I, who am good in emergencies, energetic (and "walk like seven men," I am aware), slink up to the door of my ward and stand there, dreading to go in, feeling as if I were a baby and that I would give a fortune to be well out of it. I know I have utterly mistaken my calling, as I cannot get used to seeing the entire anatomy of the human frame every time I turn around, and am altogether demented. (Now don't you see I am, by that sentence?) My only consolation is that the other ladies all feel so, too. Miss Merrill, whose mother is here, Miss Hill, a host in herself, and Miss Akin, all say and feel that their burden is greater than they can bear. I am glad for your sake you are not here; you could not stand it, even with those powders of Dr. Alcan. The odor is awful; the cases are all bad. I have had four deaths already, and there are forty-five dead to-day, two tents full beside the Dead House. The chapel is full of beds, and has been for weeks; Mrs. Wilson presides there and cooks for them herself. (Of course, the end of all approaches when *she* gets to work.)

You speak of the melodeon; it has never been thought of, and presume it has been confiscated long ago. We work hard, our beds are not made until we go down at "Taps." So many special diet meals are delayed at that "infernal" Special Kitchen (excuse me) till we are frantic. Dinner today for those poor sick men was served at half past two, supper at 7.30; gaslight and the "extras" still worse. Dr. Bliss allows far more latitude in beef tea and punch on our own orders and the extra diet not signed by him. Still, we are put off by those "fiends" who preside in that kitchen until everybody becomes exhausted and cross.

Officers now abound; I have five, Ward H twelve, Ward I fourteen, Ward K thirteen; they pay a dollar per day and have their meals served like the surgeons, which makes the third dinner to be prepared. Really the care and confusion is immense—I am not exaggerating. My "elephants" have arrived, three in one week: a barrel of crackers and two huge boxes from my New York brother, the boxes containing pineapples, oranges, bananas, lemons, figs, prunes, claret, sherry, brandy, etc. My brother at home sent me fifty dollars, other Boston men seventy, New York ten, and a cousin ten— one hundred and fifty dollars in all. I gave ten dollars to Ward C in memory of its "angel." Miss Israel does well there. Your "Albert" is doing fine; he is walking about. I have a chair like Miss Marsh's, that cost fifty dollars, and it is well worth it to the poor fellows.

May 31, 1864. Captain Dewey's father came; found they were from Brooklyn. Went with Sister Hill to Smithsonian grounds for a few moments. She would not allow me to invite Lieutenant Grenier to accompany us, who now convalescent, was sitting outside, though he was evidently ready.

June 1, 1864.

Mrs. Senator Lane, Mrs. Usher, Mrs. Ann S. Stephens, the authoress, with other ladies brought some strawberries, which I was glad to see my soldiers enjoy. It is clearing up generally. Ventilators were taken out. Assisted the ward master in covering the gas fixtures. Went to Dr. Bliss about No. 38's arm, as he begged me last night to have something done. On examination, Dr. Bliss said he must go on the table at once; so he has lost an arm, but is much more comfortable. No. 48 died very suddenly; he was brought in only yesterday. Lieutenant Grenier and Captain Robinson, both of the Fifth Maine, went to a private boarding house. Their company was mostly filled with men of position and education.

June 2, 1864.

There is a sudden change in the weather; it is quite chilly, and our patients feel the coolness sensibly. My boy with the amputated arm has had a chill, which always alarms me. Went out marketing in the morning and brought home a treat of strawberries, lettuce, etc., for my fourteen attendants. Five patients were transferred to New York. Captain Dewey's father gave me a bottle of brandy and several bowls of jelly which he brought with him.

Received a letter from William Dart, offering to give employment to some of my disabled soldiers, and from Leech (No. 17 so long), who has gone to Wisconsin, enclosing his *carte de visite*.

June 3, 1864. I hurried through my morning duties, as the ward was to be cleaned. Lieutenant Grenier came in, and I chatted with him at the window on my way to the "Home." He invited me to call and see him in F Street. My boy with the amputated arm is doing very well to-day. A surgeon in charge of the Second Corps Hospital called in the morning to say he brought news direct from Miss Southwick, and would come again in the afternoon, which he did. She has been his right-hand man, and he could scarcely say enough of her capability and usefulness. He is here on sick leave, and brought his brother, who is convalescing from smallpox. He invited me and, through me, Sister Griggs to take a drive to-morrow, which, considering the circumstances (versus our short acquaintance), I accepted. Sister S— sent a note to me from the heights of Fredericksburg, where the battle was fought last summer.

Not feeling very well after tea, I went with Sister Hill and Miss Putnam for an outing in the cars to get some fresh air. The ward master had the nets put over the beds, and Dr. Bliss complimented our ward again.

Lieutenant G— came to see us, and said he was obliged to accompany me to the "Home" to get one of my photographs. Dr. Sawyer took us out for a drive through the Corcoran grounds (now Harewood Hospital), which we enjoyed immensely. We drove to the Soldiers' Home, the President's summer home, etc.; passed Dr.

Stone's grounds, which he offered to the Government, and where the Seventh Regiment of New York encamped when here. Dr. S— was very talkative and pleasant, and picked us bouquets of honeysuckle and wild roses. The drive lasted three hours. On returning to the ward I found that two of my patients had each a foot taken off, and was much surprised that Captain Brooks was one of them. After tea, when suffering, I went to him and, endeavoring to forget his want of courtesy, put him to sleep by stroking his temples; as soon as he awoke I was sent for and requested to put him to sleep again; so think I shall have plenty to do if he is to be mesmerized often. The other amputations of to-day are doing well, but my placid one had another chill. No. 6 brought me a bunch of magnolia blossoms.

June 5, 1864.

Hurried through the morning duties, thinking to attend church in the afternoon, but, after waiting to have services in my ward, I found myself too tired. Four of the ladies are ill at the house, Miss Israel and Mrs. Senator Hawley with sore throats, resembling diphtheria. Dr. Bliss came down and made his inspection rounds. Took a siesta (if that term be allowable for a hospital nurse), then put on my " New York toilet," according to Sister Griggs, and went to see Captain Robinson and Lieutenant Grenier, as I promised them I would before they left. Found the captain still in bed, but hoping to leave for home to-morrow, and both exceedingly polite and appreciative of my visit. Found a very pretty bouquet of roses on my table, with the compliments of my old No. 6 (Dahle).

June 6, 1864.

Lieutenant Sabin left for his Michigan home, and one of my fourteen amputation patients (No. 17), successor to Leech, left also with his wife. There were plenty of visitors again. Weather is exceedingly warm. Lieutenant Grenier came down early to spend the forenoon, and bade us adieu with many expressions of thanks for himself and Captain Robinson. When I went to see about No. 12's dinner I found him failing very fast—in fact dying. I sent away his beef tea, etc., and went for the doctor to see if anything could be done for him. He was delirious, but I think knew me, as the last rational thing he said was he wished to have me give him his dinner, and afterwards he took my hand and put it to his lips. Poor fellow! He asked me a few days since if I kept the address for a letter to his parents, so in case anything happened to him I could write to them in Paterson. The ward master came to relieve me, as the attendant was too much engaged; he told me to go to the house, as he knew this was the time I usually went, and, besides, the man was so delirious I could do him no good. A severe thundershower detained me a few moments, and when I returned he had been carried out.

The father of my boy with the amputated arm, about whom we are so anxious, arrived to-night. A sad meeting it was, but he was thankful to find his son alive. Lieutenant Crosby hobbled down to my desk this evening —a little lonely, I imagine—and asked if I knew of a Shakespeare that he could get. He seems to be as fond of reading as his aunt, Mrs. Ingersoll, widow of the Attorney General of Maine.

June 7, 1864.

A sudden change in the weather again, it being quite cool. Although not feeling well, I nevertheless went to market for eggs, as I am giving two of our patients port wine and egg three times a day.

Sent No. 6 to find the brother of No. 12, who died yesterday; but, as th brother is lying severely wounded at Campbell Hospital, they could not tell him the sad news. What a burden of grief for their parents! Dr. Bliss examined No. 11's leg and advised him to have it amputated, leaving to Dr.

Sand myself the task of reconciling him to the operation. I talked to him till he smiled through his tears; tried to be brave and think it was for the best, although it was unexpected to him and, in fact, to me, as I supposed it was doing well.

Mrs. Governor Morgan made me a long visit, and brought a jar of pickles. Miss Merrill fainted this morning, and is quite ill. Some one sent a quantity of roses, and Lieutenant Crosby assisted me to arrange them. As he has not required much attention, I was surprised at his effort to make himself so agreeable. Captain Dewey rode out in Sister Griggs's rolling chair, and Captain Brooks is more tractable.

Went to the armory for the first time. Could scarcely realize before that it held such a little world of suffering. Found Mr. George Wood and Sister G— calling on Mrs. General V Hawley, wife of the Senator from Connecticut, who is lady nurse in charge. Dr. Van Slyck was unusually polite, and entertained me a while. I went to the third story, and was received by Dr. Kincade. I was taken around his ward, and there found Charlie M., one of our old patients, an attendant, although he limps yet. When I returned I found our boy No. 34, in whom we are all so much interested, was bleeding. No. 6 and I both flew after Dr. Stuart and the officer of the day. Am fearful he will not survive the night. Gave some wine to his poor father, who looked wretched, scarcely knowing where to turn. No. 11's leg amputated, and is now quite comfortable.

June 8, 1864.

There is a vacant place, as I feared, and the poor father could only grasp our hands in mute despair. Made meal gruel of that which Fanny Dart sent me, fortunately having a little left for my own breakfast and Miss Merrill's, who is better.

The wounded were brought in. We received one patient, Captain Reynolds, Acting Assistant Adjutant General on General Stedman's staff, on whose arm an operation was performed immediately after dinner. The ward master quite unwell, and went out for fresh air. As No. 6 was engaged with them during the "resection," I remained in the ward waiting upon everybody until nearly five, when I became exhausted. Captain Brooks's cousin came in with strawberries and dinner for two, and fussed in our and other wards all the afternoon. Made some more of my good gruel and sent some to Miss Israel in my cup with flags; sent also some to No. 11, being the only thing he has kept on his stomach to-day. (I fear he will go like the rest.) It seems to me an almost hopeless task to begin the usual system of medical treatment in such a condition. Made some cornstarch to treat my captain, but found it more of a task than I imagined over a gas stove. Just as I was leaving the ward, having been on my feet most of the day, a troop of ladies from Willard's Hotel came with strawberries to treat the hospital, with which, as usual, we were obliged to submit to their fashionable airs and want of sense. As an operation was going on in the dining room, they could not have dishes, to distribute themselves, and, having been to all the other wards, they were getting tired of it all, and left me to take charge of the distribution. I covered and left them until I returned to give out the special diet. Had just reached my room in the house to rest a moment when

Lieutenant C came in. Sister Griggs entertained him until I was dressed. He is still waiting orders for the "front."

A new patient was admitted yesterday (a hospital steward) who plays the piano very well.

June 9, 1864.

Found the spirits of ammonia ordered last evening had the desired effect on No. 11 and quieted his nausea, so he was able to take a little stimulant and seems much brighter. Received a letter from Sister Southwick, who has reached White House Landing on the Pamunkey River. Mrs. Governor Morgan paid me another visit and brought fresh eggs and fine large strawberries, to which I do not object as she does not worry me about dispensing them. Also an amiable elderly lady, Mrs. Grisley, came with her son, brought beefsteak, rolls, and coffee with accompaniments. This enabled me to treat all my patients in the ward at dinner, which was abominably late, and minus the beef-tea; nobody can tell why.

Captain Reynolds is from New York, and is exceedingly modest and considerate. His father is wanting something constantly, though very anxious not to make trouble. Succeeded in writing to Sister Southwick.

Called at the chaplain's a few moments to see Lieutenant Colonel Millett, who has at last arrived, wounded, but, am happy to say, only slightly in the lower part of his left arm. Dr. Baxter is with the Fifth Army Corps, which accounts for Sister Southwick's change of base.

June 10, 1864.

After dinner went out shopping, bought a table for Captain Brooks, wine for Captain Dewey, and went to the Sanitary for india-rubber rings, etc., for the soldiers; on my return found three more officers in our ward, one captain and two lieutenants. No beef-tea, and everything about the officers' diet in utter confusion. Wrote to No. 12's father and enclosed some of his hair and their letter and some money.

June 11, 1864. Feeling very wretched I sent for Antoine to bring my breakfast. Did not go to the ward until ten o'clock. Miss Read's servant brought me a letter from Sister Southwick, who is living in a tent; very interesting, and written while she was waiting for her breakfast to cook. No. 15, whose old father has been so devoted, is not improving, and is fearful of typhoid fever; but No. 11, whose limb was amputated, doing finely. Nos. 3 and 44 cannot last long. Went out after tea with Miss McClellan to market and for a diary to send to Sister Southwick, to which I added a note. Miss Israel returned from the Soldiers' Home, where she has been spending a few days to recruit. Miss Merrill has also gone to Mrs. Hall's, where her mother is stopping at present.

June 12, 1864.

Was too weary to get up and remained in bed until ten o'clock, when I felt much better and was ready for my day's work. There was one death toward evening, No. 44, a young German, who could scarcely speak English, so was obliged to have other German patients to act as interpreters. He was too weak when he came in to have his leg amputated, which was in a frightful condition. The church bells and the pleasant cessation of the street cars alone reminded us that it was the Sabbath day. It is hopeless to think of going to church, and there is too much confusion in our ward to hold services. Four new patients were brought in about noon; many more in the hospital, and hundreds on their way. Weather is quite cool.

In Ward A, among the wounded, are the colonel, major and adjutant of the Twenty-fifth Massachusetts, and the lieutenant colonel was left on the field. The colonel brought in the flagstaff with a very small piece of the flag under which they had fought so bravely. Received a letter from Miss Fox to Sister Southwick in which she says that her brother, Lieutenant Colonel Fox, was wounded again and is in a hospital at Chattanooga.

June 13, 1864. Mailed a letter to Sister Cornelia. No. 24, who came in yesterday, died suddenly. Found a friend of Miss Griggs at dinner (Miss Franky Johnson from Guilford), who is engaged to a brother of H. Ward Beecher, colonel of a colored regiment in Florida. She is here endeavoring to get a pass from Secretary Stanton to go to Hilton Head to meet her betrothed and have their marriage consummated. Mrs. Senator Lane and her sister, Mrs. General Wallace, came to see me; had not met the latter since her marriage. In the evening I went to the National Hotel to return their visit, No. 6 coming for me at nine. Garrett Davis (son of the Kentucky Senator) came in with others.

June 14, 1864.

Lieutenant Gibson is delirious; I sent a telegram to his wife. No. 30 is very low. Had a severe headache and was obliged to go to our "Home" soon after dinner. Too ill to take my tea. No. 6 came down and I sent him for a pail of hot water and mustard, but as the pulsatilla relieved my head, handed it over to Sister Griggs as a luxury.

June 15, 1864.

Ill in bed all day, but after taking some gruel for dinner felt better. Received a box of old linen from Captain Dewey's father. No. 6 came down to report. I was sorry to hear that Lieutenant Gibson died in the night and No. 30 this morning. Sent to the chaplain to have him send telegram to the former's wife. My fever patient, No. 15, whose old father was with me and watched him so faithfully, will not live through the night.

A meeting with speeches is now going on before the Patent Office; a band is discoursing music, rockets are going off in all directions, and beautiful fire-balloons are ascending from the Smithsonian grounds—all in honor of President Lincoln's renomination. It is a fine moonlight evening, too.

June 16, 1864.

Weak, but succeeded in getting dressed and waited until ten for Antoine to bring my breakfast, which came at last. The toast was very nice, but the butter had dripped into the tea and I had to take a little elderberry wine to supply its place. On my way to Ward E called to inquire after the lieutenant colonel, who has been confined to his room for the past three days, feeling very much neglected. Found four vacant beds since yesterday, and No. 3 passing away rapidly. He is Mr. Alcock, of New York, an assistant editor, and who was in Judge Phillips's office; the latter has, by letter, sent him a great many friends. My fever patient (No. 15) died at six o'clock this morning, and his father could not speak to me, though he bustled about making preparations to leave.

Mrs. Colonel Farnham came to see if she could do anything for No. 3 just after he had been carried out. Her husband is of the Seventieth New York. He was formerly in the Mexican War, and she told me had been wounded over thirty times. Wrote two letters concerning patients, and glad to have them off the list of unanswered ones. After tea went to the Smithsonian grounds for a half hour with Sister Griggs. Mr. Charles Tibbits made me another visit.

Miss McClellan is quite ill and obliged to keep to her room. Very warm weather. As our ward was being cleaned I spent part of the day with her at the "Home." Dr. Stuart is confined to his room and Lieutenant Adams, from Livingston County, New York, showing some unfavorable symptoms. I sent for Dr. Bliss, who advises him to have his hand amputated. The poor fellow seems much depressed, but he still tries to be cheerful. He is glad to have me come and talk with him, and said he would not talk about wounds when I came to see him, "but of something pleasant," for which unusually considerate remark Sister Griggs predicts he surely will not live. Commenced a letter to Miss Platt.

Dr. Tumey of Ward G came in to see our patients, and if he came often I should lose mine (patience) altogether.

June 18, 1864.

Lieutenant Adams alarmed us by showing decided symptoms of tetanus (lockjaw). Dr. Bliss was notified, and his arm was soon amputated. I suddenly came to the determination to witness it, if I could summon sufficient nerve and have company. Sisters Griggs and Israel with myself were present, and my curiosity was satisfied. Miss Israel felt faint, left for a time, and returned. I remained until they were tying the arteries, when, finding my limbs losing strength and a sickness and trembling coming over me, I thought it prudent to leave. I made my way slowly to the ward, but was obliged to sit for some time with camphor that No. 6 handed me. The ward master accompanied me to our house, but Sister Griggs never wavered to the end.

After dinner I went to the President's grounds for an outing—to hear the music and to enjoy the green grass. Received a note from Mrs. Captain Daggett about a soldier from New Bedford, Mass., who did not receive his letters enclosed in one to Dr. Bliss, fearing I might have left. Answered it in the evening. The hospital steward, our new patient, gave us some beautiful music; he arranges very pretty variations. Lieutenant Adams is no better. He knows me and spoke once, so pleasantly, since the amputation, saying, "Now you can write to my sister, if you please." His brother has been telegraphed for.

June 19, 1864. No hope for the recovery of Lieutenant Adams. Found three letters in the post office for the soldier in Ward Q, one of the extra tent wards, and had the pleasure of taking them to him. Sent letter to Mrs. Daggett with good news to his mother. Inspection was held at ten o'clock. Received a good home letter from Sister Guile, who is at Yonkers. Called to see Lieutenant Colonel Mullett, who is now improving. Was astonished to see Jobes (my first ward master), Gorman, and Perry walk into the ward. Jobes came to Washington on transports with the recruits; as his descriptive list had an error, he is obliged to give two months more of service to the

Government. Had a short religious service in the ward after dinner by a gentleman from the Sanitary Commission.

June 20, 1864.

Miss Low is quite ill. Found a vacant bed, as I feared, and Lieutenant Adams is relieved from his sufferings. Jobes spent the night with Patterson, and to-day he and Gorman left after dinner to return to Concord, N. H.

Mailed a long letter to Sister Platt. Gave Jobes a nice flannel shirt, and sent his wife Longfellow's "Children." Gave Antoine Mrs. Dibble's socks and sent his letter of thanks (which was very expressive) undercover to Mrs. Clapp, of Yonkers. Miss McClellan brought a fine treat of cherries from her home, which tasted like those from the old Quaker Hill trees. After tea went with her to the Smithsonian grounds for a short time, but found it damp. She told me of the sad procession yesterday, the funeral of the operatives who were killed by the explosion at the Arsenal on Friday. There were seventeen hearses and ambulances and over a hundred carriages, and the operatives' former companions (women) walked to the Congressional burying ground.

June 21, 1864.

Had a headache to day. Very warm. After making out diet went to our "Home." Miss McClellan brought me some toast and tea, but Lieutenant C called and I was obliged to make a hurried toilet without taking it, though soon returned after going to the chaplain, who relieved my mind about Lieutenant Adams's remains, he having received a telegram from his brother. Took leave of Lieutenant Colonel Millett, who left for home this evening, then went to bed again and made unsuccessful efforts to sleep, as the flies, the heat, and a headache kept me awake. Received a letter from Sergeant Jennings's sister, who wishes to come here as a nurse.

June 22, 1864.

Went to ward about ten o'clock and am still weak. Lieutenant Adams's brother came, with whom I had a long conversation; was quite overcome when I spoke of his wishing me to write to his sister. Miss Griggs received a letter from Sister Southwick, who was on a boat with the medical purveyor with the " Hospital Stores," all moving on they knew not where, until a place was decided upon for the new supplies. This was by the pontoon bridge over which our army has just crossed, near City Point. Went with No. 6 to look once more on Lieutenant Adams, and put a little bouquet of roses in his hands; regretted to find they had taken him away ten minutes before.

Miss Marsh made her departure on the evening train. Spent part of the evening with Miss McClellan, who introduced me to Dr. LeGrin, who visits her ward every evening. I find he is the physician that lived at Mrs. Gleason's house in New York, and I believe Dr. Fesnonder must be the party we met there; he is Dr. Socarraz's friend.

June 23, 1864.

Captain Brooks's stepmother came. Sister Griggs and I went home with Miss McClellan to dine. I enjoyed the dinner immensely, everything being so homelike and pleasant. Her brother Fred, a lawyer, was our escort home.

To-day is one of the warmest days of the season.

June 24, 1864. It is exceedingly warm and dusty, having had no rain for weeks. No. 2 is failing. Was grieved to hear of the death of Grafileman's son at the Stanton Hospital. Poor man, he could scarcely tell me about it; he came soon after with paper and envelope and asked me to write a few words to his wife, which I did and sent it by the morning's mail. Finished and mailed my letter to Lieutenant Adams's sister and answered Miss Francis's note. Miss Low left for a retired boarding house on the opposite side of the river to rest. Sister Griggs treated Dr. Banister and myself to a water ice, which was refreshing to our dust-filled throats.

June 25, 1864.

Went with Sister Griggs to have her "vignette" taken. Omitted to mention yesterday the reception of a letter from Lieutenant Colonel Fox. Lieutenant C— came in and spent an hour. Patterson received a letter the first of the week from Kysor, so long our "dresser"; he lies wounded in a hospital at Chattanooga. The weather is hot, and I am unable to do anything after dinner but breathe.

Cousin Tibbits spent the evening with me. He brought a bottle of bay rum, claret, and lemons, and gave us a little music. I remained a while after "Taps" as No. 2 was breathing his last.

June 26, 1864.

Sunday. It is as hot as ever, but a refreshing shower in the afternoon cooled things a little. Answered Miss Jennings's letter and also Will Dart's. Had two of my patients carried out in the air on their beds.

June 27, 1864.

There was another thundershower, for which we were grateful, and a change in the weather. The papers said last week was the hottest June they have had in New York for years. Captain Lippe is a very pleasant gentleman. No. 11 very weak, but hope the change in the weather will benefit him.

June 28, 1864.

Devoted myself to the ward all day, as No. 11 is failing rapidly. Wrote to his wife and to the colonel of his regiment, who is in town. Received a few lines from Sister Southwick, who reports having been quite ill, and is now at City Point. Weather again quite comfortable.

June 29, 1864. No. 11's sister has arrived. Took an order for the Sanitary Commission for india-rubber rings, etc., to Dr. Bliss for his signature, which he copied and filed away, to be sent some time by his orderly instead of by No. 6, as I hoped (we have secured the privilege of ordering things from the Sanitary Commission, which we particularly appreciate, since we have heard from the president of the commission that our surgeon in charge has requested them to honor our signature, which they are perfectly willing to do). Went with Miss Merrill in ambulance to accompany Sister Hill to railroad depot, as she made her departure this evening. Went to the Capitol grounds to hear the music, but our seats were too distant from the music stand for us to enjoy it. Craig, attendant No. 3, made me a beautiful cross.

June 30, 1864.

There was a beef-tea riot, and I openly declared my rebellion to the surgeon in charge. Captain Dewey has left us. I slept in a tent. Had tea with Miss McClellan and Miss Merrill.

July 1, 1864. Very warm again. Wrote a note to Dr. Bliss before sending my "order" to special diet kitchen, and he said it would be furnished, but when No. 6 went for it he was again refused. I wrote a second note to Dr. Bliss, saying I proposed giving up my ward at once. As he has referred my communication to my surgeon, the latter can attend to it entirely after this. Went with Miss Griggs and Dr. Banister to call on the Yatemans.

July 2, 1864.

Melting weather. A new patient was brought in during the night—Captain Schoffer of the Thirty-first Maine. He is wounded through the shoulder and his spine and lower limbs are paralyzed. As he cannot live long, I wrote immediately to his sister. Went with Sister Griggs to hear the music; the shower had cooled the air a little, so it was quite enjoyable.

July 3, 1864.

Captain S died during the night, and No. 11's sister remained with him all night. Had a headache, and went into the house until dinner. Informal inspection was held very late, just as I reached Ward E. Read an hour to Captain Lippe after dinner, a beautiful allegory, "The Distant Hills." Went to Ward A in the evening to hear some music. Sister G introduced me to Lieutenant Randall, of New York, whose wound across the neck has paralyzed his arms. He is very interesting, and gave me a full account of his experiences after being wounded. He was turned over twice by his friends and heard them say, "He is dead, poor fellow!" while unable at the time to speak. He has a wound also in the leg.

July 4, 1864.

A beautiful day, with a pleasant breeze. Gave each of my attendants a dollar for a holiday treat, which seemed to afford them much pleasure. Wrote out my list of patients since the last engagements. I remained in the ward to let No. 6, my orderly, and as many of the attendants as possible go out. The hospital gave them an extra dinner, and I made chocolate and treated them in the afternoon, and stewed my last jar of dried cherries for their tea. Didn't go to the house until five o'clock. After tea accompanied Miss McClellan home, where we had ice cream. Misses Merrill and Griggs, with Drs. Robbins and Ritchings, soon followed us. It was a pleasant evening.

July 5, 1864.

The ward was comfortable. No. 11 is holding his own, which is quite wonderful. Went out shopping with Sister Griggs for farewell presents. After tea went with her and a gentleman who visits her ward to see the stones brought for the wonderful Washington Monument, which stands in an unfinished state next to a cattle yard but we failed to get to it.

July 6, 1864. Went on the avenue and bought a present for the ward master, the dresser, etc. Received a letter from home with the astounding news that Carrie and Adolph have sailed for Europe, which makes me a little homesick. Went with Sister Griggs again to see the stones collected for the Washington Monument. They are in a small building, in the enclosure, which is a dreary spot, as there is no grass. Only the monument in its unfinished state can be seen. Many of the blocks are exceedingly interesting. I returned perfectly exhausted, but after a little tea and a visit to my ward went to Ward A to hear Misses Thomas and Yateman's music. Miss Capen and Mrs. De Quandre called.

July 7, 1864.

Exceedingly hot to-day. Sister Griggs left, and Dr. Banister is also in the same train. Wrote the following "epitaph" for Sister Griggs *a la* Chaplain Jackson, and gave it to her before her departure:

EPITAPH

I know not why I am left behind,
Unless it is to pen
The epitaph of Sister Griggs,
And prove myself her friend.
She was a girl so wondrous brave,
She never feared a "riot";
She spake her mind (she was not blind)
About the "Special Diet."
From Boston town, of course no clown
But very wise and clever;
Was loud in praise of Boston ways,
But could not live there—never.
Though kind to all, both great and small,
She never did forget
Her wit to use, and well abuse
"The New York toilette."
But she has gone, our grief forbids
To speak but in her praise;
Her heart was right, her talents bright:
"God bless her all her days."

ARMORY SQUARE HOSPITAL, July 7, 1864.

Sister Griggs is to stop at Philadelphia, and expects to meet me in New York. The Misses Capen and Mrs. De Quandre left in the same train.

A slight shower after tea prevented Sister "Mac" and myself from going to her home. Played piano for the ward.

July 8, 1864.

Arranged my private closet under table in the ward preparatory to leaving. Miss Israel is quite ill. Pay day for the men. Received a letter from Sister Southwick, who is still at City Point, which is a miserable place, their camp being in a sand bank. They are almost suffocated with the heat and clouds of dust and sand which the wind blows in upon them. Made a call in Ward A in the evening, and Lieutenant

Hooker, who came down to see me in the morning and anticipated the music in the evening, was very polite, as well as Lieutenant Randall, who is still unable to sit up. They are unusually pleasant men.

July 9, 1864.

Spent morning in ward framing and changing some of the pictures, etc. Received exciting news of another raid into Maryland. An order came to have every man able to carry a musket ready to leave to-morrow.

Lieutenant C came to the house for the last visit. Miss Israel still continues ill. Sang in Miss Merrill's ward my new song, "When Johnny Comes Marching Home," and tried duets with her; then went to my ward and repeated it. The general ward master came in and brought a tenor, and we had quite a musicale. Sisters "Mac" and Merrill and I had a long talk by the light of the stars (an unusual luxury).

July 10, 1864.

Sunday. Did not leave my bed until one o'clock. Antoine brought me breakfast, which Miss Lowell kindly brought in to me, expressing her regrets, etc.

Went to see Dr. Stuart, who has been and is still very ill. Found our best attendant (Philip, No. 4) was to leave us, and also an attendant from the dining room. Wrote note to ward master with his farewell present. Sang hymns with the old hospital choir (excepting Sister Platt and our Lieutenant C). Miss Israel is very ill and is delirious.

July 11, 1864. Began my packing. Another order for men from the hospital. Found only the ward master, with ward attendants—two for the dining room and bathroom. Johnny Hegeman, my orderly, volunteered, as the orderlies were to be exempt for the present. The rebels are skirmishing before Fort Stevens, formerly Fort Massachusetts, only five miles from this city.

Baltimore is in great excitement. General Lew Wallace was in command, and the fighting going on all day Saturday, but our men were obliged to fall back, as the enemy was superior in numbers. Miss Israel is better. Went to see Dr. Stuart after dinner; found Mrs. Ramsdell there, who informed me that she and Mr. Ramsdell thought of going North this evening also.

Received present of a beautiful workbox from my ward master, with a very appreciative note, which quite interrupted my packing. As Miss Thomas did not come and my audience did, Miss Merrill and I were obliged to entertain them with an attempt at a few favorite songs. After "Taps" sat on the chapel steps with Sisters Merrill and McClellan, in the moonlight. Our nerves were too overwrought for us to separate, and we were wondering what news the morning would bring. As we were returning we were called out again to hear the band from the Sixth Corps, which passed here to-day on a forced march and returned to treat us, playing most beautiful music for a half hour. Part of the Nineteenth Corps, from New Orleans, also passed; in fact, all day troops have been hurriedly massing to protect Washington.

July 12, 1864.

The bridge over Gunpowder River, sixteen miles from Baltimore toward Philadelphia was *burned*. The 7.30 A.M. train yesterday was attacked, the passengers ordered out, and the train then run on to the bridge and burned. This afternoon the "extras" say a few miles of double track between this city and Baltimore were torn up, so I am a fixture for the present. How Sister Helen Gwill exult that she is the other side of the "Rubicon."

Finished packing for the present. Received a letter from Sister Southwick, who has returned from the "front" ill at Alexandria with Mrs. Sawyer, and wishes me to come and bring her to Washington. No. 11 is again failing. After tea went to the Sanitary Commission rooms, when I found that Mr. Knapp and the chief clerk were in New York. After "Taps" went with Sisters Helen and Mac to Smithsonian, where Misses Lowell and Ware had preceded us, to see the shells from the Smithsonian Tower; but as they came down and reported only "signal lights" to be seen, we felt too weary to attempt to climb so many flights. Professor Henry's daughters came to the door and were cordial.

July 13, 1864.

The rebels have retreated, but many precious lives have been sacrificed. Major Jones of the Sixth Maine, just returned to his regiment from a furlough, was killed; his term of service would have expired in two days. Sent Sister Southwick's former No. 6 to get a pass and go to Alexandria to see her and report how she is. He succeeded in getting one through Miss Read, whom he met at General Anger's office. She advised him not to stop for my letter, which I had written for him to take, and came herself to make an apology, which I was obliged to accept. He found her very weak and threatened with fever. Troops are constantly passing. A train is to leave for Baltimore this evening.

Dr. Stuart is worse, and has erysipelas in the face and head. Spent evening with Miss McClellan, where I found her surgeon, Dr. Robbins, and Mr. David Burr, his father's partner, a very agreeable gentleman.

July 14, 1864.

After breakfast I was obliged to regulate ward matters (as the ward master had been watching with Dr. Stuart all night, for the fifth time, and had retired exhausted), which I did expeditiously. Went to Dr. Bliss and reported the state of things, and to see if he did not consider it necessary to detail an especial attendant for Dr. S, then to consult with Sister Mary McClellan about going to Alexandria. She promised to make out my "diet requisition." Went to Massachusetts rooms for brandy to take with me, then for a pass to the provost marshal's office, where I met Colonel Wiswall again, through whom I obtained it. Returned too late for twelve o'clock boat. Went to the ward to see No. 11's sister, as her brother died during the night, worn out with his protracted sufferings; then hurried to dinner and took the one o'clock boat. Was so weary that I took off my bonnet and went to sleep in one corner of the ladies' salon.

Found Sister S— better than I expected, but very weak and glad enough to see me. Forgot to say that the lieutenant of the guard would not permit me to take my bottles on the boat (the city is so strictly guarded), as they were not mentioned in my pass; but he kindly kept them until my return in the five o'clock boat. Reached home at 6 A.M. Took my tea, then went to see Mr. and Mrs. Ramsdell about going North. Called on Miss Yateman, who returned with me and went to the ward, where she sang and played for an hour—such a boon to the weary patients in bed. A colonel from Ward A, with his wife, Lieutenant Hooker, and some other ladies came in, and after the colonel's wife left the colonel sang; Miss Goodrich also sang some of her plaintive airs. Arranged the night medicines, as Patterson was out, and came home glad enough to retire.

July 15, 1864.

Went to see Miss Read (who is fussy enough to put even Job out of patience) at the Washington House, corner of Third Street and the Avenue. After keeping me waiting nearly an hour, was glad to see her, with bonnet on ready for Alexandria. I informed her she would be obliged to have the bottle of brandy in her bag mentioned in her pass, and insisted upon her getting an alcohol lamp arrangement also, which Sister S— needs so much. Went to Brady's gallery to get President Lincoln's picture, and found an album to suit me.

Lieutenant C— came; said he commanded a skirmish line last Tuesday evening, when the rebels thought to gobble up some cattle, about six miles from Chain Bridge, across the river. They drove them off, and a few of our men were wounded. When he left, as I was hurrying to dinner, a lady came (she was some connection of Miss Southwick's) to see if she could not be brought to her house. Found Mrs. Colonel Lowell at the table, who, as I unlocked the gate for her one evening, recognized me very sweetly duly 16, 1864. Our ward at present is very quiet; only a few of the patients (the most severe cases) still in bed. Captain Constantine Lippe, of the 188 Pa. Vols., who would not consent to have his leg amputated, after weeks of suffering lying on his back, losing flesh and strength, as he knew he must until the crisis was passed, is now gaining. His fine physique and good health have borne the strain. We have four young men carry him out on his bed into the open air, where he is to remain two hours, and I have now time to read to him. A bookseller supplies the books, and he reads constantly. It was for him I was obliged, personally, to make a raid on the special diet kitchen for beef-tea, which they would not give my No. 6 without an order.

The railway trains are running again, but are so full; it is impossible for me to get through such a crowd. Sister McClellan's father (Assistant Postmaster General) is to see me in the car (with the railroad company's key, next week, before the hour for leaving). That will be too late to see Sister Griggs before she leaves for Brooklyn, which I regret so much.

July 20, 1864.

The day has at last arrived to bid adieu to my ward and its absorbing duties, now realizing, reluctantly, how my life has been rounded within it for eight months. So with an inexpressible regret to leave even a few whose watchful eyes and patient smiles would bid me stay, though with an unspeakable longing for home and loved ones there, have given them my hand in good fellowship, and over a glass of native wine made my good wishes to Captain Lippe, my brave Philadelphian, and Captain Brooks of the Twelfth New Jersey Volunteers. *WILL I EVER RETURN?*

THE END.

Get more great reading from BIG BYTE BOOKS